ERIE COUNTY FAIR

A NOTE ABOUT THE PHOTOS…

Remember that old adage… "A picture is worth a thousand words," well that couldn't be more than true with the photos we had to work with in creating this piece. Everyone involved learned a considerable amount about the Erie County Fair by just looking through the visual images from the past and the present.

Although it is impossible to label every photo in this book, we need to give credit where credit is due. The photos compiled come from a medley of talent brought on to capture the Fair's moments each year.

Ellen Taussig's photo:M.P. Myers Photograph
Photos inside come from the Erie County Sheriff's Office, The Sheff Studio, Merrill Matthews, the Buffalo Historical Society, Network Photography, Angel Art Ltd., and Robert L. Smith Photography.

Many of the faces in the photos remain nameless, but they are the reason for the success of the Erie County Fair and Exposition in its first 160 years.

AUTHORS
ELLEN TAUSSIG 1840's-1989
LOU ANN DELANEY 1990's
MATTHEW TREMBLAY 1990's

RESEARCHERS
REBECCA STRUM
DEE ZEIGEL

EDITOR
LOU ANN DELANEY

ASSISTANT EDITOR
HOLLY SMYCZYNSKI

COVER DESIGN
HOGARTH DE LA PLANTE

DESIGN/LAYOUT
KARIN ACHENBACH

PHOTO RESEARCHER
DEE ZEIGEL

ADMINISTRATOR
VOLPINI & ASSOCIATES

PRINTER
STERLING SOMMER

Reflections of
AMERICA'S
County Fair
1841-2000

Written by Ellen Taussig

THE ERIE COUNTY AGRICULTURAL SOCIETY
Sponsor of the Erie County Fair & Expo

Our Mission

The basic purpose of the Erie County Agricultural Society, sponsors of the Erie County Fair and Exposition, is to preserve and enhance the agricultural and historical legacy of New York State. The Fair serves to fulfill appropriate aspects of the agricultural, educational, entertainment, and recreational needs of Western New York, and where appropriate, those of the United States.

ACKNOWLEDGEMENTS

A special acknowledgement must go to Paul C. Laing, who in 1989, was the Fair Manager who commissioned retired Buffalo News Reporter, Ellen Taussig to write the majority of this manuscript. Without his foresight and Ms. Taussig's talent and interest, this book would not have been possible.

Appreciation is expressed for the encouragement and support of the late Elizabeth Willett, former head of the Reference Department, Buffalo and Erie County Public Library, for her initiation and suggestion of this book; also to Rebecca Strum, researcher for Ms. Taussig for her able assistance.

A heartfelt thanks for the devotion of the many Board of Directors, staff members and volunteers throughout the years who have attended to researching photos and identifying them. In the early 90's, a debt of gratitude goes out to Russ Marquart and Diane Barber who kept this vision alive and on the burner. Director Emeritus George Hebard, Atty. who drew the agreement together. Blasé Pasqurella, a long-time friend and employee who tirelessly lent a helping hand to all. Blasé's own collection of "Fair Memorabilia" and recollection of names and dates made our job a lot easier. In the late 90's a new generation, many of whom were newcomers to the Fair but on staff, revisited the challenge including my assistant, Holly Smyczynski in the Marketing Department who inputted the entire manuscript with Danielle Pengelly for proofreading, to a talented intern from Franciscan University of Steubenville in Ohio, Matthew Tremblay who's major in English and Journalism helped me tweak the final chapter of the nineties and created the chapter titles, Paul Ranney, who patiently clips every news article for us to work from. To our Historical Building volunteer manager, Dee Zeigel who saved the day with her historical knowledge and tenacity to shake the trees for obtaining the vast majority of photos from the archives and traveling the county to identify them. Not to mention our greatest cheerleader of this project, Alice Say, Treasurer of the Creative Arts Department for her outstanding records, not to mention her foremothers records that had enough material for a book of their own. For the Board of Directors who with blind faith trusted our judgement and saw the value of capturing the history of many of their forefathers and their forefathers. The Society and I owe special, special thanks to Mrs. Joyce Laing, widow of Paul C. Laing and Kay Lietzan, both very giving Directors who at the drop of a hat would come running to pull or identify photos, or proofread our final steps. To our Fair Manager and a dear friend, Dennis Lang for supporting this effort by presenting to the Board of Directors, sweating out the deadlines with us and for the encouragement and pat on the back to the very end.

As for the design of the cover, Hogarth de la Plant (Hoagy) for his instant creativity in capturing 162 years into 11"x17". His talent and humility makes him a wonder in the commercial art world of Western New York.

To Karin Achenbach from KDesigns of Williamsville, NY, without your commitment to excellence and patience of the design of each page, this project and labor of love should not go unnoticed.

Thank you to Volpini & Associates for overseeing this project of this size with us.

To you the reader, I hope that this book enlightens you and your family and remains with you for many years to come. If you are one of the millions of fairgoers that have walked through that iron gate on the cover, we sincerely hope that your visit was as memorable to you as it was to us to bring it to you.

Lou Ann Delaney

Project Manager, 2001

TO READERS

When one paints a picture of 150 years, one cannot
use a small brush. Apologies are extended to any and all –
human, animal or bird omitted from this canvas.
It is the hope of the painter that she has at least caught
highlights.

When tillage begins, other arts
follow. The farmers therefore
are the founders of human civilization.

                              Daniel Webster

Foreword

The Erie County Fair, held on the Erie County Fairgrounds in the Town of Hamburg in August, grew to such proportions that by the latter part of the 20th Century it undisputedly called itself "America's Largest County Fair".

But like many of the "largest" or "greatest" in our country, its beginnings were modest. Before the first shovel of earth was turned in Erie County to start building the Erie Canal on August 9, 1823, the spirit for an agricultural exhibit had been raised among urban and farm dwellers alike.

While Erie County was still part of Niagara County, Buffalonian Joseph W. Moulton sent a letter to County Postmaster Augustus Porter on August 5, 1819, asking him to circulate a proposed constitution for the founding of a County Historical Society.

Response was so favorable that on September 14, 1819, the Niagara County Agricultural Society was founded in the Court House at Buffalo. When Niagara County was divided into Niagara and Erie Counties in 1821, the Society was renamed the Erie County Agricultural Society.

Most notable in the annals of the Society's first fair in October 1820 was the entry of a Merino ram. Call him unruly, recalcitrant or just plain ornery, he made an impression —- he captured the spirit.

He was brought through the unfenced forest and moors of the Indian reservation by horse and wagon from the Hamburgh farm of Dr. Cyrenius Chapin, the Society's first president who also was the first physician to come to Western New York state. The first fairgrounds were in Buffalo on Main Street near the Terrace that overlooked the waterfront. The Fair was declared a success, considering the sparse population of the county and the lack of any road system.

In the words of 17-year-old Orlando Allen, who assisted Dr. Chapin in his varied interests:" "The day was fine, the entries quite numerous and everything passed off to the satisfaction of all concerned." (the Merino lamb perhaps was the exception). A b all closed the ambitious event.

A second fair was held in the fall of 1821, now under the suspices of the newly-named Erie County Agricultural Society. But the state of the economy of the area and the difficulty of

transporting livestock over nearly impassable roads caused a decline of interest among area farmers. The Society foundered.

In 1841, however, interest in the Erie County Agricultural Society was revived. It was reorganized with the stated purpose of "the promotion of the Educational, Horticultural, Mechanical and Manufacturing interests of Erie County." Lewis F. Allen, a large Grand Island landowner and experimenter in livestock breeding and fruit raising, was named president.

Another Fair was held October 5 and 6 in that year in Buffalo. It was the start of continuous fairs sponsored by the Society until 1943, a year it was exempted because of World War II.

The next year, however, the Erie County Agricultural Society again became active and another fair was held in Buffalo. It was traditional that the fair continued to be held in Buffalo until 1850. Then it shuttled between Aurora, Lancaster, East Hamburgh (now Orchard Park) and the Cold Spring area of Buffalo. The New York State Legislature passed a law covering agricultural societies in 1855 that required they be reorganized on a uniform basis.

So, on June 4, 1856 in the same court house where the first society was founded, the Erie County Agricultural Society once more was organized anew.

George W. Tifft of Buffalo was elected president, along with vice presidents John S. King of Amherst and William Hambleton of East Hamburgh; George W. Scott, treasurer, and Hiram C. White, secretary, both of Buffalo.

Directors elected were Erastus Wallig of Willink, Austin Kimball of Williamsville, A.K. Humphrey of Holland, Myron Stilwell and William Hambleton of East Hamburgh and Aaron Riley of Aurora.

The society then leased a site on Indian Church Road West Seneca, where the fair was held for nine years.

In 1868, after holding fairs in Springville and the Cold Springs area, the Erie County Agricultural Society moved to its present site at Hamburgh (the "h" was dropped in 1877).

The grounds contained a racetrack operated by the Hamburgh Road Drivers Association.

After purchasing the Hamburg 12-acre property in 1882, additional land has been acquired until today, the Erie County Agricultural Fair covers 260 acres of land.

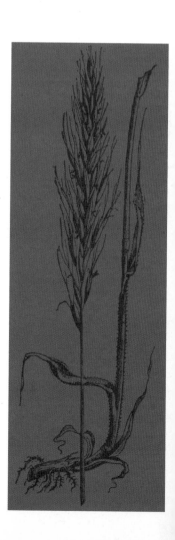

Society is Reborn
Chapter 1

"What God hath wrought!" were the words sped over the first telegraph line, from Washington to Baltimore on May 24, 1844.

And early sounds of the feminine voice were heard in July 1848, as Lucretia Mott and Elizabeth Cady Stanton led the Women's Rights Convention at Seneca Falls, New York.

By 1840, the Holland Land Company had brought thousands of farmers and their families to Erie County, Western New York – 40,000 of them. Well-cultivated fields and spruce farmhouses spread across the land.

Leading citizens, proud of their newly incorporated City of Buffalo, with its population of nearly 20,000, also had reached out and acquired large farms in towns like Aurora and Grand Island, where livestock and fruit growing experiments were conducted.

Such community leaders, with others in the countryside and towns like Hamburg, Holland, Wales, Eden, Boston and Amherst, in 1841 revived an earlier Erie County Agricultural Society, which in 1822 had foundered on nearly impassable roads and consequent lack of interest by farmers. Lewis F. Allen, owner of "Allentown," a 600 acre farm on Grand Island, was elected President. So, a third Erie County fair was held in October 1842, on the Delaware Avenue grounds of Dr. Ebenezer Johnson, former first Mayor of Buffalo.

The weather was good. Allen displayed "a noble herd" of cattle, and Cyrus Belknap, also of Grand Island, showed splendid yokes of Oxen. William Mann of the Hydraulics exhibited a mammoth sow, weighing 800 pounds. Prizes for winter apples, pears and squashes were carried off by Benjamin and William Hodge. Manning Case, who won the first premium for carrots, reported planting his seeds May 21st or 22nd and cultivating with a hoe. Premium-winning crops produced per acre: Indian corn, 57 bushels; oats, 67; barley, 42; carrots, 1,124 ½; rutabaga, 1,000; beets, 1,280. The Ploughing Match, which drew at least 2,000 persons, was won by Peter Curtiss with his chestnut team. The ground allotted was a quarter of an acre, and the time an hour and a quarter. Curtiss finished in 51 minutes.

In the "Household Manufacturers" section, Mrs. Ira McCall of Aurora demonstrated that the spinning wheel was still in use in the smaller towns by her display of homespun flannel, while Mrs. M. Conklin of Clarence knitted a "superior" pair of silk stockings.

Mrs. Allen won the honey exhibit. They made a great cheese at Hamburg. For many years it was considered the prize cheese in the State.

"There was no peculiar method used in making the article in question," notes H. Perry Smith in his History of the City of Buffalo and Erie County. "It was simply first-class cheese (which won the premium at the State Fair first held in Buffalo in 1848)." It was widely copied; however, cheese factories finally absorbed the private dairies, and by 1884 there were none which manufactured cheese for sale.

"Acting on the principle, that the publicity in all… proceedings was beneficial," Society as it will henceforth be designated, began to furnish information to the Buffalo press.

A great many farmers attended the 1843 Fair held in Buffalo.

"It is to their attendance and interests that the efforts of the Society must be directed," emphasized Robert McPherson, president. "It can and must be drawn into the proper shape…We must go on."

Sheep exhibited were more numerous than ever, and a bit of pride and competitiveness creep into Society' outlook."In the long wooled sheep, we generally make a better display than the State show has for two years past," the president said. "If the State of New York means to beat us in 1848, when they visit us, they must do their best."

"A better display of butter and cheese than at Auburn (Cayuga County Fair) was shown, but our dairymen can and will do better."

Elias Howe would not invent the sewing machine until three years later, and "Household products were not so numerous as we wish."

Judge Thomas C. Love, County Surrogate, took the first premium for his farm and was awarded an extra diploma.

Shipping rates on the Erie Canal were lowered from $100 to $3 a ton, as railroads began to lace Erie County, opening wide markets to farmers.

The Almanac is considered irrefutable. But the Erie County Agricultural Society's third annual fair in 1846 proved its fallibility.

A calendar used by the Society in determining the dates for the fair listed Tuesday and Wednesday as October 11th and 12th respectively, instead of the 10th and 11th correctly.

New handbills issued only a week before the fair failed to reach all parts of the county.

"In consequence many animals and products were prevented from coming, or did not arrive until the second day," noted Judge Love, now president.

"The committee, however, permitted every thing to enter at whatever time it arrived…"

Weather was not "on the whole, propitious." It rained part of each day.

Nevertheless, the executive committee was pleased "to witness so fine a spirit, as seemed to animate everybody on the ground," and with the increase in entries and farmer memberships.

The consensus of the Society now was that " a thorough dissemination of the facts is alone required

1840's

to be spread among our fellow citizens, to make our annual fair a great jubilee to our whole population."

Society's executive committee made some new plans when it met in March, 1847.

A leading one was: "That whenever any member of the Society shall win one or more premiums, amounting in the aggregate, or solely to two dollars or more, he shall receive in part payment, thereof, either the 'Genesee Farmer,' for the year 1848, at the price of fifty cents, or the 'American Agriculturist,' for that year, at one dollar."

"We believe, that the circulation of the agricultural journals of this state, as premiums at our exhibition, has the tendency to promote a taste for agricultural improvements, and a greater interest in our own association," stated president Orlando Allen.

It also decided to permit sale at auction of all articles exhibited at the fair at its conclusion. And it agreed to write the Horticultural Society to unite in the Fair.

"It is unquestionable that our society has affected great good," reported Mr. Allen. "In sheep and swine, there has been a most decided improvement in this county...Our cattle are seldom of the unadulterated, thriftless native stock, though cattle of very high grades are not yet very numerous.

"The breed of horses has greatly improved within in a few years, both in size and shape, resulting partly from the greater demand for good horses, both in Buffalo and for eastern markets, and also from the general prosperity of the farmers themselves."

Oxen exhibited at the 1847 fair were "creditable."

The address by the Hon. George W. Clinton together with a "a brief and frank statement of the only objects of our Society" was forwarded to every farmer in the county.

Those objects: "the advancement of agricultural science, the consequently increased progressiveness and value of each farm, and the work of each man who labors upon the farm, and the greater comfort of each farmer and his family."

William N. Bennet presented a seven year old cow, who the first week in June gave 310 lbs 3oz. Of milk, from which 12 lbs 10oz. Of butter was made. The New York Agricultural Society Fair was held in Buffalo in 1848, and the Erie County Fair was not held in deference.

And nearby, on the Buffalo waterfront, Joseph Dart, an imaginative and enterprising merchant, had raised the first steam-driven grain elevator. It replaced stevedores in toting grain cargo from the developing fields of the West to storage holds, eventually transforming Buffalo harbor into the largest storehouse of grain in the world.

END 1840's

Going to the Country
Chapter 2

The Erie County Agricultural Society held its fair in the country for the first time in 1850.

It was a wise decision.

"Owing to little interest on the part of the people in the country towns," regretfully reported Secretary Aaron Riley, "the Society had almost become extinct…"

More than 8,000 persons attended the fair at Aurora and the exhibition as a whole "far exceeded any of its predecessors since the organization of the Society."

Entered in competition for $550 of premiums were 133 cattle, 89 horses, 73 sheep, 23 hogs.

Some good specimens of wagons, oxbows, horse-rakes, stoves, etc. were shown in the Mechanical Department.

Messrs. Jewett and Root of Buffalo presented "some splendid rakes and parlor stoves, equal if not superior to any offered to any community."

A bed quilt worked by Mrs. Alonzo Rayner of Clarence attracted much attention.

With remarkable foresight, President W.H. Sotham, Esq. declared that "the high price of labor is now a drawback to agricultural improvement," but that "the time will soon come when labor will find its level and its real value."

"The immense number of immigrants will afford facilities for work of this description," he prophesied, and thereby render the land more productive, and thus enable us to support them, and their industry receive proper award."

The earliness of the season, extreme heat for several days previously and an "unlucky selection of exposed ground" at Lancaster diminished the size of the 1851 Erie County Fair.

"What there was, however, was good," reported W.R. Coppock, Society Vice-President, adding a bit of philosophy:

"As exhibitors under such circumstances are of the active and right kind, their commodities are likely to be good also." Except the State show, "there had never been so fine a display of agricultural implements."

"The Messrs. Mason and Lovering of our city, having recently

established one of the largest and most extensive establishments in the State, made a grand display," noted Mr. Coppock.

"This establishment…will work great good to our farming interest, by furnishing the tools needful, which alone can do the good work."

1850's

Fruit culture was receiving increased attention throughout the country, and Society believed that "no section of our State is better adapted to the successful growth of fruit generally, than Erie."

Society felt it had good reason to be encouraged with its prospects in 1852.

"The farming interest seems, to some extent, to have awakened from its lethargy, and is determined to enjoy the means of improvement which are placed within its reach," stated President Amos Chilcott.

Milch (milk-giving) cows, generally a mixture of the native and Durham, were thought to be the best ever exhibited in Erie County.

Superior specimens of French and Spanish Merino sheep were shown by the President. Much improvement in the quality of fruits and vegetables was evident. Poultry was abundant of all shades and colors, "from the highest hen fever variety down to the old speckled hen."

A spirited plowing match was held during which, sportsmanlike, "the best kind of feeling prevailed throughout the contest." The "taste, ingenuity and industry of the ladies of our County" in the Domestic Manufacturers exhibit was proclaimed fully established by President Chilcott.

Splendid tents with streamers waving in the breeze animated the 1853 Fair on the racecourse at Cold Springs.

Highly conspicuous was the "very extended" display of poultry, embracing all the various breeds from Gallus Giganteus to the Queen Pheasant, bantam breed, to feather, color and spot.

"It has been said," Society proudly reported, "that no exhibition in this State for number, high blood and extreme beauty, would at all compare with this collection; $75 per pair was the asking price for some of them."

A great novelty was displayed in tented Floral Hall where among the fruits, flowers, houseplants, etc. were specimens of Nemosperma Balsamina or Balsam apple, a native of India presented by Mr. A.I. Mathews.

The fruit which "beggars description" is six or seven inches long and one and a half to two inches thick, of a rich golden yellow roughed on the surface somewhat like the summer crook-necked squash.

The Allen B. Wilson improved patent stitching machine, an "elegant and ingenious affair," was at full work, making 12 to 15,000 stitches per minute "with the greatest exactitude," a successor to the Elias Howe sewing machine. Elias Howe had invented the sewing machine eight years before.

Some dozen oil paintings by Mrs. Warren Granger were displayed, as well as watercolors by Mrs. J.G.D. Stevenson. Evans and McDonald showed daguerreotypes.

Haircloth embroidery was exhibited by Mrs. H.A. White. On the more utilitarian side, "a beautiful collection of baths and improved household conveniences" were contributed by Messrs. Hampton and Grattan.

The Hon. George W. Clinton, a descendent of George Clinton, first Governor of New York State, who delivered the address said: "Your occupations, Gentlemen, are calm and ennobling such as wise and good men, in all ages, coveted. They have a charm for young and old, present a happy alteration of necessary labor and delightful ease, and favor growth in mental stature and moral strength…"

"To the noble employment by which you prosper, and to your country, you owe another duty – the elevation of agriculture both as an art and as a science. Art and science are working most marvelous changes in the practice of the farmer…and now, if I read aright, the rotary digger promises to supersede the plow. It seems almost incredible that this venerable instrument would fall into disuse…"

For the first time in Society's history a small admission fee was charged non-members. Finances were tight. A note of pessimism crept into the report of Society President John W. Hamlin on the 1854 Fair at Aurora.

"The County being divided in the center by the new wild country known as the Buffalo Creek Reserve, renders the Exhibition a local one when removed from the city of Buffalo…more distant parts of the County entering but few articles."

1850's

The show of horses, however, was very good. The products shown, "though inferior to ordinary seasons, in consequence of the drought, were nevertheless, equal to the adjoining counties."

But no funds were contributed to the Society except for member's fees. Balance in hand was $174. 1855 was a watershed year for the Erie County Agricultural Society. The New York State Legislature on April 14, appropriated $8,000 "for Agricultural Societies in the several counties (Erie among them), and the State Agricultural Society, for the promotion of agriculture…"

The new law required that all societies reorganize on a uniform basis. Society enclosed nearly four acres of ground in a beautiful grove in East Hamburgh for its fair in 1855, inside of which were erected pens for sheep and swine and arrangements for cattle and horses.

A hall over 100 feet in length and about 20 feet wide accommodated tables for dairy products, fruits, flowers, needlework, paintings, etc.

Dynamic yet whimsical, Horace Greeley, who had founded the New York Tribune in 1841, arrived to dedicate Society's 1855 Fair.

In her memoir "In the Long, Long Ago," of 1949, Grace Clark Thorn of Hamburgh describes him as "A regular Beau Brummel with his dark, tight trousers tucked into his high heeled boots, velvet vest, long light coat…tan hat – a sort of plush affair with extremely broad brim…"

Mr. Greeley told the intent crowd, "No farmer can afford to produce weeds. They grow, to be sure, without cultivation; they spring up spontaneously on all land, and especially rich land, but though they cost no toil, a farmer cannot afford to raise them…

I am accustomed, my friends, to estimate the Christianity of the localities through which I pass, by the absence of weeds on and about the farms. When I see a farm covered by a gigantic growth of weeds, I take it for granted that the owner is a heathen, a heretic or an infidel – A Christian he cannot be, or he would not allow the heritage which God gave him to dress and keep, to be so deformed and profaned."

With foresight Mr. Greeley declared:

"As more enlightened views of diet prevail, fruit is destined to supplant the excessive quantities of animal food that are consumed in this country. This change will produce better health, greater vigor of body, activity of mind and elasticity of spirits…"

In conclusion, Horace Greeley warned that "nature won't be cheated. She will repay all you bestow upon her with interest, but she insists that you shall furnish her the materials out of which she elaborates crops, and that you shall remove all obstructions to the freedom of her operations."

A number of ladies showed their skill in horseback riding in 1855, "which," commented the Society with a dash of chauvinism, "however profitable or commendable it may be, created a good deal of excitement and interest."

B. Maltby presented a sample of winter wheat from a stated yield of 39 bushels per acre, while William Hambleton offered a specimen of corn gleaned from a crop of over 100 bushels an acre.

A few, "very nice" carriages and buggy wagons were displayed.

Thus, June 4, 1856, in the same Buffalo Court House on Washington Street where the early settlers founded the first Society thirty-five years before, the Old Erie County Agricultural Society was reorganized.

Its business and objectives "the promotion of Agricultural, Horticultural, Mechanical and Manufacturing interests of said County."

Officers were to be a President, two Vice-Presidents, a Secretary and Treasurer, all of whom would compose a Board of Managers.

1850's

Any resident of Erie County might become a yearly member for $1.00, a life member for $10. A handsome gold-tooled leather book was purchased for the recording of minutes.

Lithographing of a certificate of life membership, with suitable decrees and inscriptions was authorized.

Society then leased a lot on Indian Church Road in South Buffalo for a fairground for a term of ten years.

And Despite the unfinished state of the grounds and two very windy, dusty unpleasant days, the attendance at the 1857 exhibit was "fair" and receipts nearly $500."

A note of elitism crept into requirements for premium competition in 1858, as a Superintendent of the Cattle Department was appointed, among whose duties were:

"Particularly to examine the thoroughbred stock to see that no animal is entered as such, without first exhibiting an undeniable pedigree showing the purity of the blood."

Premium for the best stallion was set at $10.

The sole privilege of "victualing" (providing food supplies) the 1859 fair was granted to D.H. Burt of the Sulphur Springs Hotel.

The first Atlantic cable was completed, in recognizing the value of widespread communication, Society ordered 1,000 show bills for the Fair. The price of admission was raised to 15 cents.

End 1850's

1850's

Home Sweet Home
Chapter 3

The Civil War cast its shadow over Western New York in the first half of the 1860s.

But the Erie County Agricultural Society, plagued with insufficient interest from farmers, rain and drought, did its best to keep up its spirit.

It was not until 1868 that Society admitted its plight, and by confession and a new Fair location, gained a renewed lease on life.

Minutes of Society, before or after the War, bear no mention of it, but Underground Railroad stations were prevalent throughout Western New York. Secrecy was considered the best policy.

Yet Erie County contributed over 20,000 men to the War, many undoubtedly farm men and boys, and sustained over 4,700 casualties, wounded or missing.

As Abraham Lincoln became President in 1860, Society sought subscriptions to erect "a trotting and exhibition course" on the fairgrounds in South Buffalo, where it had met the past eight years, and cheerfully reported "more and more interest manifested every year by farmers and citizens generally."

But despite buildings and lumber on the grounds and the new half-mile trotting track, "worth one thousand dollars at least," Society still owed $673.

Classes however, were more numerous, as follows:

3 horse classes, 4 cattle classes; 2 sheep (fine wool) classes; 2 sheep classes; 2 swine and poultry classes; 1 fruits; 1 flowers and plants; 1 grain and roots; 1 vegetables.

1 farm implements; 1 domestic department; 1 household manufacturers; 1 castings, hardware, etc.; 1 miscellaneous - 21 classes in all.

Society vacillated between awarding silver medals and cash premiums, settling on the latter.

A family ticket was issued at $1.00. Two buildings to provide refreshments on the grounds were rented. A police group was hired at $1.00 a day, or night.

The first transcontinental telegraph line spanned the Atlantic.

The Homestead Act which granted free family farms to settlers, and the Land Grant Act, providing for public land sale to benefit agricultural education, precursor of the New York State University Systems, were approved in 1862.

Perhaps encouraged by Federal interest, in 1864 Society Treasurer George W. Scott reported with spirit:

1860's

"We hope before long to be able to stand in the front ranks of agriculture in the Empire State. It is slow work but sure…We have the means to accomplish it if we are willing to think so."

Receipts and expenditures balanced at $1,326.25 in 1865, but indebtedness remained - $433.00.

As Robert E. Lee surrendered at Appomattox, and lilacs prepared to bloom in Western New York, the cortage of Abraham Lincoln wound through the awakening countryside.

Society, restive and dissatisfied, resolved that the next fair, 1866, be held "in a town fitting up the necessary grounds, and offering the best pecuniary inducements."

The new grounds of the Union Agricultural Society at Springville, a strictly agricultural district in the central part of the county was chosen "to try the effect of a new locality."

For the first time, the fair was scheduled to run four days.

Indicative of the deep roots of the Erie County Agricultural Society in the soul of Erie County was the fact that the Springville grounds were the site of a farm established in 1812 by the Dygert Family, a descendent of whom, Robert W. Dygert, DVM, became Chairman of the Board of Society in the late 20th Century.

The farm enclosed a half-mile racetrack known as the Springville Driving Park, one of the oldest racetracks in New York. It was a harbinger of the place horse racing would occupy in the future of the Erie County Fair.

Durham and Ayrshire cattle and working oxen stood out, with entries of swine, "superior to any before exhibited" at the Springville Fair in 1866.

The newly-formed Ladies Department, under the supervision of officers chosen by the women of the Society themselves, displayed "everything which tends to make a home pleasant."

Several types of sewing machines, as well as fine specimens of house and church organs, graced the 1867 fair.

Prizes of $8, $5 and $3 were authorized for "the team that shall plow ¼ acre the best and in the shortest time."

Heartening to farmers across the land was news of the founding of the Grange, a national fraternal association designed to protect farmers' interests.

Society's annual meeting on January 9, 1868, was a historic one.

The Hamburgh Driving Park Association offered Society "the use of its new half-mile track and grounds, with office buildings and seats – free of charge – for holding its next Fair."

A heated vote was close – for moving to Hamburgh 18 – for remaining at Springville 17.

On September 23rd, 24th and 25th 1868, the Erie County Agricultural Society held its first Fair at Hamburgh, where today it continues to meet today.

1860's

Of the 1868 Fair, Secretary R.C. Titus reported:

"Our efforts were not entirely without success; but owing to the fact that the Society for the last five or six years had been gradually losing the confidence of the farming community, and had become nothing more than a town affair (and a very slim one at that)…"

Opening day the "windows of heaven" opened…it rained all three days.

Undaunted, the Hon. Hugh T. Brooks Wyoming County, who delivered the annual address said:

"Improved agriculture by providing for material wants has always opened the way for intellectual, social and religious advancement. The progress of the plow, from stick to steel, has marked the real progress of nations…

You may safely judge any people by their agriculture. Elegant mansions have grown from good fertilizers…when buildings take imposing shapes, and all furnishings and surroundings indicate competence, wealth and social culture – you may be sure there is good grain or grassland there, and it has been well tilled!"

By the 1869 Fair at Hamburgh, Secretary Titus was able to proudly crow that attendance was "the largest since organization of the Society", receipts "about double" of last year, and "a general interest and good feeling was manifested by all present." There were 510 entries and gate collected about $1,000.

Commented the Buffalo Commercial Advertiser at the three day conclusion:

"It is gratifying to know that the Fair was a success, showing a revival among farmers and others of the interest which rendered these occasions so attractive and beneficial in former years…"

"The trotting park and the grounds adjoining are admirably adapted to the purposes of the Fair, and the buildings are arranged to the best advantage."

As the golden spike driven at Promotory, Utah, marked the junction of the Central Pacific and Union Pacific Railroads to complete the Transcontinental Railroad, the Erie County Agricultural Society itself, was at least headed down the track.

End 1860's

1860's

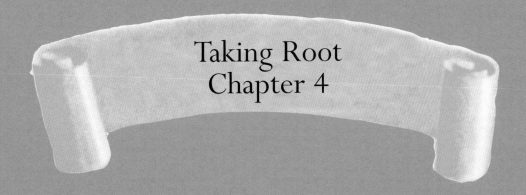

Taking Root
Chapter 4

The world seemed smaller in 1870, as the Trans-Atlantic Cable joined the United States and Europe.

As the International Bridge across the Niagara River connected Erie County and Canada, railroads rolled Buffalo towards its Golden Age. Forty years before "Tom Thumb," the first practical American-built locomotive had steamed down the track.

The Erie County Agricultural Society shared in the expansion. The strategic decision of the Society to accept the Hamburgh Park Driving Association's offer of its grounds as a Fair site, free of charge, was the turning point:

"We are pleased to learn that the entries at the fair have been much larger this year than before, and that more enthusiasm has been manifested by residents throughout the County," reported the Commercial Advertiser in advance of the Fair's opening in 1870, the year the Government Weather Service, later the United States Weather Service, was established.

The layout of the Fair became more impressive. Stretching 96 x 24 feet, the Agricultural Building alone drew 350 entries.

Exhibits ranged from fine buggies, wagons and sleighs by Bangert Brothers of Angola (who also won a diploma for the best two-seated covered carriage – (with or without the fringe on top?) – to the display by Messrs Fowler and Son of Buffalo, with straw cutters, corn shellers, root cutters, spokes, etc., and climaxing with F.S. Hunt of Water Valley's farm rollers, plows "and other implements of improved manufacture."

A multitude of farm machinery had been developed before 1860, including the reaper, mower, iron plow, disc harrow, grain planter and straddle cultivator.

Farmers, innately conservative and wary of the cost of such "mechanics," as they were called, were slow to accept them.

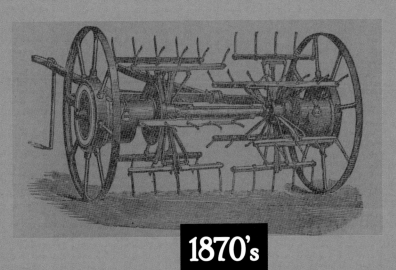

1870's

But during the Civil War, as the government called thousands of farmhands to military service, they were forced to buy them.

Ultimately, farm machinery would cut the time necessary to produce the country's ten major crops by 48 percent.

On the distaff side, the Ladies Department, 64 x 24 feet, was hung inside with quilts, blankets and rag carpets made by hand.

The varied displays showed such diversities as the prize winning ten yards of homemade all wool flannel by Mrs. P.W. Powers (premium $2.50), and Mrs. J.C. Newton's breakfast shawl ($1.50), through exhibition of a case of bird nests "of her own hunting" by Miss Maria Salisbury.

In a day of tub and washboard, the Triumph Washing Machine exhibited by Messrs Isaac Erb & Son of Buffalo received welcoming interest, while the National Bee Hive, an invention of Mr. E.B. Redfield of White's Corners, was "well designed to produce straight combs, thus insuring easier handling; and to protect the bees from the frost and cold." It was termed a valuable improvement.

The Committee on Awards was cautious in visiting the section occupied by a display of sewing machines from Grover & Baker, Wheeler & Wilson and Empire Machines "all apparently doing good work and each surrounded by its own friends and admirers."

Said the Daily Buffalo Courier: "The Committee forbear toexpress an opinion of the relative merits of these machines for fear their lack of experience in fancy stitching might embarrass the managers of these labor saving machines, and lead astray and confuse those desirous of making purchases." As competitors for premiums increased, it became necessary for Society to set restraining rules and regulations, such as:

"Competitors for premiums must be members of the Society. A payment of $1.50 to the Treasurer constitutes a member..."No animal, after receiving a first premium, shall again compete for a premium in the same class...

"No mechanical or household productions, which have received a premium, may be presented again for competition..."

"Each person offering grain, roots, or seed, must produce a fair sample...for exhibition or examination, and must, at the same time, produce and leave with the Secretary, a true statement of the quantity raised, by weight or measurement; also of the measurement of the land on which the same was respectively grown."

In his address X.A. Willard, Esq.,warned that, "It was a mistake for the children of farmers to look down on farming; that there is no other business which yields so certain a reward and that only five in a hundred succeed in mercantile life."

Mr. Willard, with marked foresight, called for "schools and colleges as necessary, and such as will give their pupils practical experience in the field. It is equally important, he said, that farmers' daughters should be properly educated as well as their sons, that they may make good farmers' wives."

The comments of the speaker on this latter point, the Buffalo Courier noted, were "quite telling," and elicited a round of applause. Women, long in the background of farm life, were inching forward.

In 1871 Society turned from rhetoric to more commercial pursuits.

Secretary Titus reported to the New York State Agricultural Society in explanation as follows:

"It has been the aim of officers of the Society to devise some means whereby the agricultural and manufacturing interests of the county might be made to subserve the wants of the people at large, and impress them with the idea that their interests are identical and reciprocal."

To this end the long-established custom of an annual address by a prominent speaker on the last day of the fair was discontinued. Gone were the declamations on the Almighty and the heart rendered stanzas of verse.

Instead a general sale of stock and implements at the exhibition was held, " in imitation of the practice long-established in England and Canada."

"Our expectations were more than realized…" reported Secretary Titus, "for the number of entries of articles for competition was greater by forty percent than for the last ten years."

In 1874, feeling the need of permanent ground under its feet, Society appointed a five member committee, instructing it "to examine relative to the advisability and feasibility of making a permanent location plan for the holding of the annual Fair…"

At the annual meeting of 1875, President C.R. Carey reviewed the history of the Society, and in contrasting premiums offered in its earlier days with those given currently, showed striking evidence of its prosperity. Some examples:

In 1855, D.G. McCracken won $4.00 for the best stallion. J. Cook of East Hamburgh took $10.00 for the best in 1875.

V.R. Carey received $4.00 for the best bull in 1855, but Robert Dygert of Springville brought home $10.00 for his, twenty years later.

Winter wheat gained a $4.00 first in 1855 for W. Maltby, while V.R. Carey of Boston netted $6.00.

Seth Fenner won $4.00 for four cheeses in 1855, while two decades later, S.K. Benjamin won $5.00 for two factory cheeses.

Fifty cents was aquired by Mrs. M.W.B. Bull for a tumbler of currant jelly in 1855, but Mrs. J. Hawkins of East Hamburgh doubled that in the mid-1870.

The 1874 figures had been impressive: Receipts, including the annual $453.37 of State Appropriation, were $2,083.06; expenditures for premiums and expenses, $1,683.06, giving a balance on hand of $400.00. While not a startling amount, it was written in black ink.

Encouraged, Society pushed on and accepted a joint offer from H.D. Rand and Frederick Thompson to match their $150.00 to construct a barn, believing that "such a building is greatly needed and will prove itself a source of revenue to the Society…"

A Building Committee was appointed to erect it. Conditions of partnership gave Society "complete control of the barn during the days of the Fair only," the other owners to occupy it the rest of the year.

Most important and satisfying of all was the entrance in April, 1875, of Society into a contract with the Hamburgh Park Driving Association to lease its grounds, where it had met without charge for the past seven years, for the annual Fair at $50 a year, "as long as the Association holds their own lease."

1870's

The relationship of the two parties was to last 125 years.

It seems in order to picture the setting of the Fairgrounds at the September fair of mid-1870.

"The grounds," said the Commercial Advertiser, "which are about ten miles southwesterly of our Main Street (Buffalo) are unsurpassed by convenience and beauty. Sloping gently upward from the public road, the plot, enclosed in a substantial board fence, is about equally bisected by the main avenue leading up from the entrance.

To the left is a half-mile track, firm and smooth, with just enough pitch to give a good send-off and home stretch. A stand with seats for spectators is shaded by a thick growth of pines.

On the north side of the avenue is a grassy margin, beyond which the native forest growth has been retained. The ground on this side slopes down to a shady dell, at the bottom of which a spring of pure cool water gushes from the bank and flows away in a light little rivulet.

In addition to the barn, a music stand had recently been built."

People who did not drive to the Fair could now take the Buffalo & Jamestown Railroad there. Two trains ran daily, leaving Buffalo at 8 am and 4 pm, approximately an hour's ride. Omnibuses ran between the depot and the grounds.

But many drove. The Buffalo Daily Courier describes the scene at the Fair on September 15, 1875, of which George H. Addington was Marshall – a fair with 25 classes and 45 judges:

"The day was pleasant, and the air extremely clear and bracing, and a gentle breeze from the lake made matters altogether lovely…"

"Every available spot on the ample grounds was filled with horses and vehicles; the barns and fence corners in the vicinity were crowded with those unable to find hitching room within the enclosure, and from early dawn to sunset the roads were lined with comers and goers."

Society began to operate its own dining hall, superintended by Mr. Jerome Titus, where "all who have occasion to reinforce their true inwardness will find here an attractive and wholesome bill of fare."

As the "inspiring strains" of the Gowanda Brass and Angola Brass Bands played on, the mid-70's Fairs offered increasing style and variety. "I'll Take You Home Again, Kathleen" was a current favorite.

In the Vehicles and Farm Implement Department, Messrs. John Kinney & Sons of North Evans displayed a double park phaeton, a double family carriage, single covered phaeton, three spring market wagons and three spring iron-clad express wagons, "all of excellent make and finish." The double phaeton won first premium ($5.00).

In horses, J. Cook of East Hamburgh placed first with the best five-year-old stallion ($10.00), stallions incidentally were quartered in the new barn; Ransom Jones, West Hamburgh, showed the best fat oxen ($6.00), and J.D. Yeoman of Aurora excelled with the two best ewe lambs ($2.00).

In the Grains, Roots and Vegetables Section, C.E. West of Buffalo triumphed with the best acre of barley, W. Partridge with the top acre of oats.

A notable entry in the Agricultural Hall was a large collection of garden vegetables from the Country Farm, submitted by Superintendant Charles Loeberick, "fair samples of the vegetables raised by pauper labor," as the Commercial Advertiser put it.

Mr. B. Baker of Potters Corners entered 67 varieties of apples, while Mr. W. Sprague of the same place showed 90 specimens of pears.

The thriving Ladies Department displayed Mrs. Silas Potter of Abbott's Cornes' fine lot of houseplants, which attracted particular attention as she had no greenhouse or conservatory, and the plants wintered either in the parlor or the cellar.

Among "Natural Flowers," top premium winners included Mrs. M.M. Bowie with verbenas ($3.00), Mrs. E. Johnson, pansies ($2.00), and Mrs. J.H. Hawkins, zinnias ($1.00).

In the "Ancient and Unique" Class, Mrs. H. Knapp won a first premium for a 100 year-old coverlet ($1.00).

Officers of the Fair wore appropriate badges to designate their authority by 1876.

Five superintendents presided: Daniel A. Simons over horses; Nathaniel Foote, Cattle; Henry Wheelock, Sheep and Hogs; Amos H. Baker, Agricultural Implements; and George S. Moore, Poultry and Miscellaneous.

With increasing crowds, Christopher Hambleton was appointed Chief of Police at $10.00 for three days.

Rules were tightened as the Fair progressed. In the important competition for the "Yield Per Acre of Grain," the exhibitor now was required, at the time of entry, to "make a statement under oath before a Magistrate or Notary Public," giving an explicit account of the raising of said crop...

A rope was ordered to enclose the stock during the time the Judge was present, to keep exhibitors and the public from entering, as a firm resolution was passed that "no exhibitor shall point out to the Judges the good qualities of his own exhibit or the defects of others, on danger of forfeiting his premium."

Society widened its geographic horizon in 1878, an important step. A committee of three, chaired by the President, was named "to appoint one suitable person from each town in the County, that has no representation on the board, to be distinguished as Honorary Vice Presidents, who shall serve for one year and specially interest themselves within their own towns' representation at our Fair and meetings."

A contest was held for all brass bands in the County outside of Buffalo, the winning band receiving the first premium of $30.00 to play at the Fair the following day — or lose said premium. Gilbert and Sullivan's tunes were resounding throughout the countryside.

A Free-for-All race was offered at a $150.00 purse.

As the 1870's drew to a close three premium highlights were those:

"For the best portable exhibition of the products of husbandry and mechanism of not less than fifty different articles made by any person, neighborhood, Society or Association, which shall be exhibited on the track."

A "Traction Engine" to be exhibited by F.L. Maltby "capable of drawing anything around the track, which the Society desires…" (Society was cautious: premium to be withheld unless it does what it is recommended to do.)

With 72 judges elected to twenty-five classes, a balance of $949.15 in the bank, and a Poland China Boar joining the Swine Class – life membership in the Erie County Agricultural Society was raised to $20.00.

Single tickets were twenty-five cents, and children came to the Fair free.

End 1870's

To scatter plenty o'er a smiling land,
And read their history in the nation's eyes.
Thomas Gray

Expansion, Expansion, Expansion
Chapter 5

Expansion was the Erie County Agricultural Society's banner in the 1880's, as this formerly struggling enterprise dedicated to " the promotion of the Agricultural, Horticultural, Mechanical and Manufacturing Interests" of the County prepared to take its place among the great County Fairs in the United States.

The Hamburg-centered corporate character of the Society, presided over by its staunch Board of Managers, many of Yankee stock, with its credo of thrift, was broadened by the election May 15, 1880, of newly-elected nineteen honorary Vice-Presidents from towns throughout the County 'to serve one year and interest themselves in the Fair's activities.'

Membership had long been open to and eagerly welcomed from residents throughout the county, but now representation, a stronger inducement and force, was available.

The towns were: Alden, Amherst, Brant, Buffalo, Concord, Colden, Collins, Cheektowaga, Eden, Evans, Grand Island, Holland, Lancaster, Marilla, Newstead, Sardinia, Tonawanda, Wales and West Seneca.

As asphalt began to replace planks on Buffalo streets, transportation across Erie County became easier. Two years later, South of the Border, the Panama Canal was begun.

"The most successful exhibition ever given by the Society..." said the Commercial Advertiser of the 1880 Fair.

On the third day, "the city contributed five carloads of visitors via the Erie Railroad (round-trip fifty cents), and the County surrounding Hamburg sent in wagon-loads and buggy-loads until it seemed as if the rural district population had rallied to a grand Garfield and Arthur demonstration."

1880's

About 18,000, "the best crowd ever," poured into the grounds, and by noon, with hardly an available spot in the enclosure, hundreds of teams were hitched along the fence outside.

The Buffalo Daily Courier waxed eloquent: "Yesterday (the opening day) was a red letter day in the calendar of the Erie County Fair, and the twenty-fourth annual exhibition was covered with a blaze-dazzling glory that caused the hearts of the managers to leap with joy…

"The ostentatious double carriage drawn by prancing thoroughbreds, the modest buggy and the unpretentious farmer's wagon all joined in the procession…"

But excellent order was preserved, stated the Buffalo Morning Express, "not a fight was reported, and but very few intoxicated persons could be seen, the sale of liquors not being allowed on the grounds."

"Innumerable refreshment stands had been erected to add to the gaiety and old-time festivity of the occasion, and the irrepressible and omni-present shooting gallery, California swing, sideshow and peanut man, which decoy the uneasy nickels from the purses of rural youth…" also were present.

A record premium list of more than 300 was offered, with an unprecedented 1,573 entries.

Mrs. Carlton Smith was president of the increasingly popular Ladies Department, with its 879 entries.

Highlights of the 1880 Fair were a four-year-old trotting contest; a 2.40 trotting race; a bicycle race (half mile heats purse $40), William T. Walker winning all three heats, and a "walk, trot and run" (half mile each, purse $30).

A magnificent chestnut stallion, young Ontario Chief, weighing 1,730 pounds, owned by D. W. Burt was driven by Dr. W. J. Chamberlain.

Messrs. H.C. and J. Jewett gave an exhibition with the two year old Titania and three-year-old Hamlin, and "trotted the youngsters two half miles. The colts struck a gait considerably faster than the three minutes."

The bulls, Silver and Dana, proudly led the largest herd of Jerseys displayed by Charles Abel of Buffalo – cows Mystic, Cothie, Sadie and Annie, the heifer calf Flora tagging along.

Holsteins represented by the herd of A.P. Wright, held Mahomel, Maid of Holstein, Soda, Apple Blossom, Richmond, Vina, Prince Albert and Nina, a fine two-month old offspring bringing up the ranks.

Lay's Silver Seneca Cornet Band from the Cattaraugus Reservation played to an appreciative crowd. "Silver Threads Among the Gold, " made its debut.

All of which drew this accolade from the Buffalo Morning Express:

"For several years the Society had been increasing in power, and last year it freed itself from all encumbrances and had a substantial surplus in the treasury. The Fair stands second among the many County Fairs of the State, both in point of attendance and number of entries. Kings County alone excels it, and that will, by another year, be outstripped by its western rival, should the latter continue to experience the   success of the past two years."

1880's

Receipts at the 1880 Fair totaled $3,958.17, and with a tidy hangover balance of $1,603.37 from the '70's, Society's managers now found themselves in proper shape to negotiate for the grounds on which the Fairs were held, and purchased on January 17, 1881, 12 and 2/100 acres from Marian and Naomi Clark at $200 per acre, amounting to $2,404.00, which was paid in cash, and on April 1, 1881 – 12 and 6/100 acres from George M. Pierce at $100 per acre, totaling $1,206.00 for which a Bond & Mortgage was given.

Thus the Erie County Agricultural Society, now – at last– was itself a landowner.

Courage has been a characteristic of Society down the years.

Undaunted by a mere $530.03 remaining in its treasury, a committee was immediately appointed "with power to draw plans for such buildings and other improvements as may be required, also to contract, as early as they may deem it expedient for such lumber as may be required..."

As the Fair advanced in years, the entertainment and dining facilities increased. Fairgoers wanted more than exhibits and livestock; they wanted visual and audible excitement; they wanted entertainment and hearty fare:

Such as Allen Monroe's renting space for the cigar trade – a big attraction of the time. By 1884, there were three stands with exclusive rights to sell "smokes"; W.S. Wilson's exclusive right to operate an Air Gun, and the dining hall space granted to Myron Colvin "for which he is to furnish the Society (members) 100 meals, and what more they have, at twenty five cents per head."

A Chief of Police and Marshall provided order and direction at $3.00 a day, respectively.

Groups began to rent the fairgrounds for picnics, among the first being St. Patrick's Catholic Church of Buffalo and SS. Peter and Paul Roman Catholic Church in Hamburg.

By June 1883, as Standard Time was adopted throughout the United States, Society declared itself worth $6,440.29, including 24 8/10 acres of land and ground improvements of $3,334.34.

Reflecting the enterprise of the times, the popular free-for-all race premium of $150.00 was doubled.

New premiums included those for:

One bushel of White, Amber, Spring and Russian barley and one half bushel of potatoes, including White, Elephant, Early Rose, White Star, Early Ohio's and Beauty of Hebron.

Egalitarians triumphed over elitism in the admission of two swine entries, the first of two pigs under six months old, "on which no pedigree is required," and the second, a grade (half purebred) boar and sow, with offspring under two months old.

Gentler offerings included a $20.00 premium for ladies equestrianism, and an exhibit of stuffed birds and eggs.

As 1883 drew near a close, Society considered "the advisability of procuring the right of way for a Side Track from the Buffalo & S.W. (Southwestern) Railroad to the fair grounds, and to enlarge the same by procuring more land if deemed best...provided the Railroad will lay the track for the same."

Gradually more substantial buildings began to rise on the Fair site, which now covered 25 acres of land fenced with substantial posts and boards. Water, taken from the spring on the grounds was carried by pipes, to reservoirs situated in various parts of the enclosure.

A grandstand was ordered built in time for the 1884 Fair, the bid of

1880's

Hamburg Planing Mill Co. of $2770 being accepted. A double kitchen 14-X-24 feet was erected on the north side of the grandstand, and a "mammoth" dining room was placed under it.

"The grounds were never in such splendid condition as at present," said the Commercial Advertiser of the 29th Erie County Fair in September, 1885. "The spacious grandstand, Agricultural Hall, and unique Ladies Department and other smaller buildings are among the new attractions. Indeed everything denotes renewed enterprise and success

on the part of the Association…"

The paper continued, "Good judges pronounced the Ladies Department the most attractive feature of the fair."

Some lines on this Ladies Department, the exhibits of which down the years have given perhaps the most graphic, intimate and touching picture of County rural domestic, family and personal life available.

From the inherited quilt to the pin cushion on the farmer's wife's bureau, from the hand woven coverlet to the crocheted lace tablecloth, from the flowers of the garden to the green of the house plants, nurtured against the winter cold, from superlative pies to pickles and jams - the homey panorama of daily farm life have crowded the Ladies Department Halls.

Even today, first premiums – the red, blue and gold Tricolor awards excepted – rarely run as high as $10, most are $5.00 or less. Some used to be 10 and 25 cents.

But the psychological value – a term unexplored in the last century – cannot be estimated. To the housewife, often living far from the center city and its attentions, often fields away from neighbors – the recognition, the sharing and the sense of personal achievement that such exhibits bring has been and continues to be, truly rewarding.

It was in 1885 that Hoffman & Getz constructed the Women's Department Octagonal Building for $2,037.50.

Octagonal (8-sided) churches were the latest fashion in Holland when the Dutch came to New York. The people of New Amsterdam built them, and the style continued into the 19th Century.

Eight-sided houses of all kinds from school houses, barns, carriage houses, chicken houses, bath houses and even an occasional blacksmith shop were put up.

Octagon buildings were built in more than 20 states and Canada, but the greatest number were in New York.

A new Agricultural Building also replaced the old one by 1885. (It is now the front section of the Historical Building).

Concession stands were awarded to the highest bidder, D.C. Corbin acting as auctioneer. Prices paid ranged from $10 to $62.50.

Excise Justice Read of the County Court "presided over a lemonade and pop stand with dignity and grace."

With such solid and attractive footing and 38 classes on its premium lists, Society began to reach out beyond Erie County to the Country at large.

Membership was taken out in the National Trotting Association. J.D. Yeomans of East Aurora was named a delegate to the biannual meeting of the Breeders Association in Chicago, and an out-of-towner was included among the judges, as Mr. Pees of Mt. Morris, N.J., came to judge Jersey Cattle.

A more intensive interest was taken in horses both in show ring and on track (now widened on the backstretch.)

Among a series of Stake Purses offered were those for 2, 3 and 4-year-old colts, with prizes ranging from $15.00 to $30.00, which would be doubled by the Society. Publicity was stepped up and news of the series was sent to the press and letters to breeders of fine horses.

The purse for the 3-year-old horse Stake Race was raised to $150, and that of the Free-for-All fixed at $250.00.

A medal was presented as the Herd prize, a herd to consist of one bull, 2-year-old or over; two cows, 3 years or over; one 2-year-old heifer, and one 1-year-old heifer.

The cattle exhibition listed 26 Ayrshire, 38 Jerseys, 8 Herefords, 1 Durham, 38 grades (half purebred), and 4 working cattle.

J.M. Richmond of Buffalo, who had a herd of over 40 Jersey cattle at his West Hamburg stock farm, showed one of his cows named "Well Done", 8 years old, which had recently produced enough milk in seven days to make 19 ½ pounds of butter.

Supervisor Issac Brayton of South Wales exhibited 40 varieties of potatoes, while Calvin Nicholas of Aurora displayed 50 variations of apples.

Two of the largest squashes "ever raised in Erie County," a California variety weighing 150 pounds each, were presented by O.F. Smith of East Aurora.

The "badge banner" shown by Mrs. S.M. Stuart, President of the Women's Department, composed of firemen's badges from throughout the state, were "uniquely arranged," attracted the admiration of all.

"The dancing floor and swings furnish plenty of amusement for the festive belles and beaux," reported the press.

Orson Paine of Aurora was Marshal of the 1885 Erie County Fair, which drew a record crowd of "at least 25,000."

"The Managers of the Association contemplate purchasing more land and building a mile track before another year rolls around…" reported the Commercial Advertiser at the Fair's close, "and by offering large purses in the future they will add to the number of entries in the various classes and further promote interest in the Fair."

Continual outreach for more land, erection of new buildings and better and wider personnel organization marked the second half of the 1880's at the Erie County Fair.

A keener recognition of the drawing power of entertainment attractions, highlighted by the thrilling novelty of balloon ascents; improved publicity and an increased welcoming of various agricultural, patriotic and civic groups to meet on the fair grounds reflected a maturing Society, more sensitive and open to the country at large.

Superintendents of the main classes for the 1886 Fair of which Dr. George Abbott was Marshal were: Gayer Gardner, Horses; D.C. Corbin, Sheep; A.M. Blackman, Agricultural Implements and H.P. Hopkins, President, Licenses.

A committee was formed to ascertain "if any lands south and west adjoining the Society's grounds could be bought and at what price."

Secretary Oscar Wheelock, in a subsequent report, stated that "the Clark and Newton parties who own lands on the south and adjoining Society's grounds – the former positively refused to sell, and the latter would sell for $300 an acre."

The committee then was authorized "to purchase or lease any land or lands adjoining the Society's grounds, as in their judgement may seem proper."

A. Newton sold 2 55/100s of acres to Society in September for $275.00 an acre – price $701.25. A Committee was appointed "to make any repairs or build any new buildings that in their judgement may seem necessary."

Another building for cattle, a larger dancing floor, at ($125.00), two new sheds for sheep and swine respectively, a carriage shed and chicken coops (courtesy of the National Poultry Association) were anticipated or raised, Society took out $400 in insurance for the grandstand, Ladies Department and Agricultural Hall.

In 1887, for the first time, officers of Society were paid "as high as $50.00" a year for their services. And Charles D. Wood offered an astute amendment to Society's Constitution in 1888, as follows:

"Whereas at the expiration of the term of office of the President, it seems desirable that the Society should have the benefit of their experience and advice. Therefore be it resolved that the last three ex-presidents of the Society compose a committee whose duty it shall be to act with the Executive Committee in all matters relating to the Society, but without the right to vote."

On the lighter side, the proposition of H.D. Squire to make a balloon ascension on Society's grounds during the 1887 Fair was accepted. The size of the balloonist's fee of $150.00 was indicative of Society's growing recognition of the public demand for entertainment at the Fair.

Prof. Carl Meyers was engaged to make two balloon ascensions on the grounds in 1888. The Buffalo Daily Courier gave this enraptured account of a balloon ascension and parachute descent in August, 1889, by "aeronaut" J.F. Elliott.

"The balloon, which was 65 feet high and 45 feet in diameter, was very quickly inflated with air heated by a fire kindled in a hole dug in the ground of the enclosure formed by the race track, and about 4:30 the monster was released.

From its side hung the white folds of the parachute and on a bar suspended below the balloon was the aeronaut. The atmosphere was very still. At about the height of the treetops, the air-ship encountered a slight current which carried it a little way, but it soon rose above that, and its ascent was almost perpendicular to an altitude of nearly 4,000 feet, where it seemed to become perfectly stationary.

The crowd watched in breathless expectation, and many of the women who were inexperienced in such performances manifested their nervousness.

Presently, Elliott was seen to lay hold of the parachute rigging, and in a moment more he released his grip on the balloon, which, relieved of his weight suddenly, bowed nearly over and ascended somewhat higher.

The daring man fell swiftly for some distance, but then the parachute swelled out wide and full, and gracefully as a bird descended to the earth, just outside the Fair grounds…"

The Commercial Advertiser was less impressed: "The 'professor' (apparently the balloonist had assumed the title) who went up in a balloon delighted everybody. He made a nice jump with his parachute and landed like a bird. But just why he should be called 'Prof' because of this feat is unknown. Perhaps because he says so. He didn't look any more like a 'professor' than a newspaper reporter or any other Darwinian species."

Society "granted the privilege" to the Western New York Grand Army of the Republic Encampment to hold their annual encampment on the Fair grounds in 1887; also the Erie County Farmer's Institute, and the Hamburg Fire Department.

Procurement was made of 400 large and 800 small posters for the Fair, and 100 diplomas (awards of merit) were printed.

The Orchard Park Cornet Band of 16 men were engaged. "Love's Old Sweet Song" was a popular favorite.

Stands at the 1888 Fair were a colorful and pungent maze of a tent for oysters, melons and fruit from wagons, peanut stands, photograph and shooting galleries, pinwheels, balloons and whips and notions.

1880's

Oysters were a delicacy in the 1880's.

"Exclusive of the leading hotels, there are about four thousand oyster saloons in this city," noted the Commercial Advertiser, "which dispose of from fifty to one hundred bushels a day, the average (saloon) being eight bushels."

Size is not the criterion for oysters, the newspaper insisted. Small and richly flavored Oak Island and Blue Points were most popular. It is dubious if the Erie County Fair would hold its place of preeminence today, if Society had lacked the courage of the pioneer ancestors of its Board.

Although increasing in revenue as the Fair progressed, Society continually poured its earnings back into expansion and improvements.

For example, 1887 receipts totaled $6,672.84, disbursements, $6,737.21, leaving a deficit of $64.37. Despite receipts of $5,633.46 and disbursements of $5,655.46 in 1888, Society's balance was $22.20 short.

But means always were found. A small mortgage on property was taken out. Society rode on.

Secretary C.H. Wood was dispatched, with expenses paid, to the State Agricultural Societies meeting in Albany in February 1889. With an eye to economy judges of classes at the Fair were cut from two to three to one per class, and an assessment levied "on all parties using the track for working or speeding horses, in sums sufficient to keep the track in proper condition..."

Plans were made to engage a different band for each day of the Fair.

New premiums of the latter 1880s at the Erie County Fair were for both carriage and road horses; potato planter and potato digger and manure spreader.

For a Durham Bull, 3 years or over with three of his gel, $10.00; greatest and best variety of pigeons, no less than four varieties, $3.00. Best "variety and quality" of sewing machine work to be executed on the grounds, a diploma.

End of 1880's

1880's

"And still sail on, Oh Hamburg Fair! Sail on! You Bet you're getting there!
The farmer folk with pumpkins thrashed, The city horde with pool-checks cashed,
Are stuck on you ~ as you're aware! Fear not chill winds or threat of rain;
The crowd is with you! That is plain. While there's such bloomin' lots to see
You're welcome to our entrance fee..."

The "Gay Nineties"
Chapter 6

Overflowing with enthusiasm about the Erie County Agricultural Society's 39th annual fair in 1895, the Buffalo Daily Courier burst into the above verse.

As the nation entered the "Gay Nineties," and Buffalo, its Golden Age — a lucrative braid of rails, grain, lumber and steel production — the Fair entered the "big time" in attendance and attractions, reaching a record of "not less than 15,000 people on the grounds" in a single day at the 41st annual Fair in September 1897. The Fair again was extended to four days.

The Buffalo Courier paints the scene in varied and vivid color, and en route catches the urban-rural philosophy which contributed to its stunning success:

"The exhibition itself is a typical one, "but not to have seen the Hamburg Fair" argues one, "is to have missed one of the institutions of the vicinity of Buffalo." It retains today the features that characterized it a quarter-of-a-century ago, and yet the exhibits give unmistakable evidence that the country folk, in their way, are keeping abreast of the times.

"Country fairs are much the same the world over, but with the circus they divide one of the tenderest spots in the average American's heart. They form a neutral ground on which city and country people can comfortably meet without either feeling that there will be a difference between them. All this and more is the Hamburg Fair. It is a success…"

A visiting correspondent from the publication The Orange County (N.Y.) Farmer, commented:

1890's

"This Fair is unique among the County Fairs of the Empire State. First, it is well attended, and therefore successful financially; and second, it can boost of being the most remarkable gathering of fakes on this earth…The area of the ground is about 60 acres, and it contains a half-mile race course, one of the very best in the State…"

"The displays offered to these large crowds are not to be compared with those offered by the Orange County Fair, so far as legitimate exhibits go…"

He describes the scene thus: "Entering the gates, after

depositing his 25 cent fee, the visitor sees the racecourse first of all. Next, to the right, he sees a line of tented fakes, the women with the bracelets and necklaces of writhing snakes…the horse with 'a mane 25 feet long'…the black haired albino…

In front of each fake was the foghorn, voiced, leather-lunged, clapper-jawed 'orator', inviting the visitors to enter and inspect the wonders of the tent.

The photograph gallery was rushed with business…Mixed with the cries of the fake orators were the sounds of the bell announcing another race. Some good races were run, but the man who was there to see an agricultural show could not help wondering what on earth the 2.29 ¼ of "June Bug" had to do with the agricultural problems demanding the attention of farmers of Erie County…The whole panorama suggested the midway plaisance of the Colombian exposition on a small scale…

The intelligent farmer may well ask: 'Of what real good to farmers is a farmers' fair, with less farmer than fake, fraud, game, sight and races in it? I never so fully realized the significance of this question as I did when looking on the remarkable gathering in the Erie County Fair grounds…

But there was the fair, and there were the farmers in great numbers from all parts of the country. It is one of the riddles of agricultural life, which not most philosophical of observers can solve any more satisfactorily than can the most careless of thinkers."

The Fair continued to stretch. In 1890 Society decided on purchasing additional land and widening the track. A committee was appointed "to ascertain upon what terms more land south of the Fairgrounds could be purchased to make the south line of the grounds straight."

In January 1891, land totaling 37 74/100 acres was bought at $80 an acre.

H.C. Jewett & Co. was "granted the privilege of building a barn on site chosen by them" on the Society's grounds, which barn, Society almost immediately bought for $150.00.

President H. Wayne White of Hamburg congratulated Society in 1892, on its "present flourishing condition; the improvements made the past year all paid for, and a balance left, $874.66; we have now as a good a half-mile track as there is in the country and plenty of land for enlarging the grounds," he said.

Transportation to the Fair of course was of major import.

Late in 1890, a committee was formed to interview officials of the New York, Lake Erie and Western Railroad Co. to find out if "a switch and siding could be extended to the Society's grounds from their main tracks." But Society turned down Erie's price of $4,800 to lay the track, and decided to look for some other railroad accommodations.

The decision was in line with Society's characteristic attitude of independence and good bargaining. Yankee and German stock playing its cards close to the vest.

Complaints about railroad service to and from Buffalo and Hamburg crested in 1890. The Buffalo and South-Western division of the New York, Lake Erie & Western Railroad Co., as the regional line was then called, went from Buffalo through the towns of West Seneca, Hamburg, Eden, North Collins, and Collins, crossing Cattaraugus Creek at the village of Gowanda.

Overcrowding and lateness on the return trip from Hamburg to Buffalo – an 8-mile run – on September 25, caused the Commercial Advertiser to strike out.

"The ordinary reader perhaps does not understand why the railroad treats its Buffalo patrons in this shabby manner. This is the sequel: The railroad offered to lay a switch into the Fair grounds (the Fair depot was about a mile north), if the Officers would allow them the use of the park for picnic purposes in summertime.

"The Officers refused on the ground that the buildings would be literally torn down by the picnickers, and an agreement has never been reached. Both sides are at loggerheads, and in the meantime Buffalo people are the sufferers."

A special, however, was run at 50 cents round trip.

"The trains from Buffalo were large ones and overcrowded at that," wrote the Buffalo Courier in 1895, " but the hundreds of Buffalonians drove out. The fairgrounds were almost covered with vehicles of every description, from gorgeous tally-hos from Buffalo to antique canvas-covered wagons from the Indian Reservation at Lawtons."

And when they finally arrived at the Hamburg Depot?

"Alighting from the train at Hamburg, one is confronted with the rears of a score or more alleged stages, near which are as many or more drivers and conductors howling and scrambling for passengers," reported the Buffalo Courier.

"Everything is taken good-naturedly, and the rivalry coming as it does but once a year, is enjoyed rather than otherwise by those whose lot it is to be pulled and hauled about and finally boosted –boosted is the word – up the tortuous steps into the box."

Society realized early in the 1890's that "special attractions" were an essential part of a crowd-drawing fair.

Competition in the farmer's field of agriculture and livestock was stimulating and raised standards. But farmers saw horses, cattle and crops the year-round and knew them well. In days before the transmission of sound or scene were undreamed of – something different, something strange, something chancy was sought.

Nor was this interest in the unusual confined to country folk. The urbanites too, relished such sights and sounds. The Midway or plaisance, as the French called it, was the name for it. The site of the amusement section of the World's Fair in Chicago in 1893 was so christened.

In preparation for the 1891 Fair Society asked the New York State Association of County Fairs to recommend attractions they had or could suggest for County Fairs.

"Special attractions for the Fair are one of the things that trouble the Managers more than anything else," registered Society's minutes.

A committee on special attractions was formed. Serving were Horace Landon, Edward E. Hepp and George P. Dick. It was ruled however, that "no games of chance" be allowed on the grounds.

The Program for the "Special Attractions," in addition to those of the midway at the 1894 Fair, with awards ore generous then heretofore, follow:

*Steeple Chase – one mile, first prize Silver Cup, 2nd $10.00

*Best performance of a professional coachman driving a gentleman's turnout (a coach or carriage together with horses, harness and attendants), first prize $15.00, 2nd $10.00

*Ladies Saddle Horse ridden by the Lady, first prize Ladies Sidesaddle, 2nd bridle, 3rd whip

*Running Race – Riders to change horses and the last one to win, first prize harness, 2nd blanket and 3rd whip

*Ladies Driving Single Horse, first prize silver water pitcher, 2nd gold-lined cup

* Shirt race – first prize a suit of clothes, 2nd overcoat, 3rd pair of pants.

Apparently by 1895 Society became more discriminating on its Midway:

"Some of the regular features of a County Fair will be missing," reported the Buffalo Courier. "Shellmen, ring and cane men, shooting gallery fiends and similar nuisances have been barred…that patrons may not be annoyed.

"To be sure red lemonade, striped candy and peanuts will be in plenty, otherwise it would not be a genuine agricultural exhibition."

The most popular midway attraction to arrive at the Fair in the 1890's was a troupe of Japanese acrobats and tumblers, who performed daily between heats of the races, "thus making the waits less tiresome."

"They are really the most clever people in their line that have been seen in this section of the country," said the Commercial Advertiser. One of the troupe is a diminutive specimen of humanity who is tossed about in the air by the feet of a heavier comrade. He is a prime favorite of the crowd."

Fat ladies and Circassian (Russian) Beauties, formerly barred

from the grounds, were readmitted toward the end of the century. And in the strange perversity, the public paid 10 cents to see a camel-back cow and five-legged calf.

Concessions offered a wide-range, from patent medicines, suspenders and comic song dealers' wares to whips, buttons and picture postcards.

The man with whips cursed his lack of foresight. At the 1895 Fair, he had a stack of about 1,500. Nearly every man wanted from two to six colored whips, and the whip man could have sold 10,000.

Perhaps best capturing the spirit of husbandry, the true essence of the Fair in the 1890's, was the gentle brood mare "with foal at feet" that won first place for George Andrews of East Aurora, and the fact that the young Merritt Burtin contributed 20 varieties of potatoes – he had grown himself – to the Youth Department.

There was a good deal of food besides peanuts at the Fair. In 1892, the Woman's Christian Temperance was "furnishing eatables" and Traekle's Restaurant dispensed meals under the huge grandstand.

"The vendor of cream candy warranted to remove the filling form

one's teeth on the first application," noted the Buffalo Courier in 1893, "and the ear-splitting rubber squawker (a noise-making gadget) is in the mouth of every boy and girl whose face is not already buried in the center of a two-foot slice of watermelon…"

Sellers loudly proclaimed the tender qualities of the "Coney Island Sausage" by 1897, when the Methodist Episcopal Church Society operated a refreshment stand and one D.F. Pringle, an eating house.

All of such nourishment was eaten, quaffed and swayed to the jubilance of such bands in the 1890's, as the L.A. Seneca Brothers Band "which literally murdered the air"…Smith's Silver Creek Coronet band (17 men at $140 for the Fair's duration)…the Springville Coronet Band "played sweetest music throughout the day"…the Eden Band, East Aurora Band, Lancaster Band, Java Village Band, and finally in 1897 – five bands for each fair, a different one for each day.

And the merry-go-round played on...and the tin-type gallery clicked cheerily on day and night...

In the absence of enough permanent buildings in the 1890's, tents were raised in abundance at the Erie County Fair. A large tent for the display of flowers in 1893...The Commercial Advertiser, its own tent on the grounds "where our readers will be welcomed throughout the fair"...and a large tent outside the enclosure where horses and rigs could be cared for at a small fee.

Many exhibitors also raised tents.

Horse races continued as the heartbeat of the Fair, seconded by the Women's Department, which early had indicated the Ladies Home Journal motto - "Never underestimate the power of a woman."

"Seldom is better racing seen at an agricultural fair than yesterday (September 25, 1890)," reported the Commercial Advertiser. "Of course no pools were sold, the laws of the state prohibited this, and the old turfites might be led to expect that the racing would not be so spirited on this account. But such was not the case. Every heat was a turf battle worthy of a grand circuit meeting, and contested upon its merits."

At the 1895 Fair, "the horse racing was the chief attraction of the day and the grandstand was filled to overflowing..."

"During the racing a tally-ho party from Buffalo entered the grounds, and this gay equipage was followed by a burlesque coaching party – hayseed dudes, seated on a homemade tally-ho made out of soapboxes. The 'basket' for canes and umbrellas was a wastepaper basket."

Bicycle races "open to all" were scheduled.   As to the horses themselves, an imposing equine backdrop was the 150 foot H.C. Jewett & Co. barn, which they lent to Society for use during the Fair; the new plank floors laid in the trotting horse stalls, and the freshly whitewashed railing and fences around the track and show ring.

Early in 1890's, the Commercial Advertiser commented thus on the horse department: "The leading stock farms do not enter for prizes, simply for exhibitions, if at all, preferring to give the farmers a clean sweep. This is certainly commendable on the part of the stock farm kings, but it serves to make the farmers lazy..."

The Buffalo Courier disagreed: "One of the most prominent features is the exhibit of horses, and it will compare favorably with any other in the country. The farmers in the Southtowns (South of Buffalo) are largely engaged in breeding, and many of the best exhibits were produced by them."

The importation of horses was noted: H.G. Hubbard of East Aurora had a "superb" display of Arabians, including two black and white middle mares, Jessica and Juliet, and two suckling fillies, Snowflake and Blackbird.

Among the Percherons exhibited by Frank E. Metcalf of "Maple Grove Farm," East Elma, was the famous 5-year-old stallion Alltf, a French coacher. Three other large and handsome Percheron stallions were Pic, never beaten in a French Show Ring; Chartre, an iron gray, and Voltaire, a handsome light dapple gray, with silver mane and tail.

Coach horses drawn in pairs to a wagon were acclaimed one of the finest exhibits at the Fair in 1893.

By 1897, more than 100 horses were entered in the races. "Crazy Jane," a bay mare owned by Frank Briggs of Orchard Park, won first prize in the novelty race, which involved driving a mile in 5 minutes, as nearly as possible without the aid of a watch or receiving any information from spectators. Crazy Jane finished in 4.54 ¾ minutes.

Pony racing was offered in trotting, pacing and free-for-all classes.

From the cattle barns in 1895 came the celebrated herd of Jerseys owned by Charles S. Sweet of Buffalo, which were exhibited at the World's Fair in Chicago. Numbering over 40 head, the herd, famous among all breeders of Jersey cattle in the State, was heralded as "worth going many miles to see," as was L.B. Croker's exhibit of a herd of deer.

1890's

The Guernser herd of E.C. Taylor of Lawton's Station took nine first prizes and all second and third premiums in its class. In the Ayrshires, George Tabor, East Aurora, took five firsts, five seconds and three third premiums.

The Ladies Department – as the Victoria era waned, it became the Women's Department – reached full stature in 1893. Mrs. D.R. Armstrong, president of the Erie County Ladies Club requested and was granted the naming of that September 20th, as "Woman's Day at the Erie County Fair."

The press acclaimed the department in 1890, as "the leading future of the Fair," and Society subsequently furnished flags to decorate its building.

In 1893, Mrs. S. Augusta Armstrong of Buffalo, president of the Women's Political Equality Club, read an address "on the much discussed topic of 'Woman's Suffrage.'" Men vied with the women present in applauding.

Casting modesty aside, Mrs. E.O. Cheney, president in 1895, proclaimed that year's Fair as "the best we have ever had, both in quality and quantity, in all departments – particularly ours."

By 1897, the department had enrolled 2,500 entires.

The presence of W.T.C.U. members exerted influence on the grounds, but stronger refreshments remained available at the tent saloon outside the gates run in 1897 by John Miller. Ladies racing came in too; a contract arranged with a Miss Alice Jackson for "a racing exhibition" was made in 1891.

Yet as late as 1895, the Buffalo Daily Courier waxed sentimental about the Fancy Work Department: "The gem of this collection is an exhibit of some local made honiton and point lace..."

"Erie County is fast becoming noted for its fine poultry," reported the Buffalo Courier of the 39th Erie County Fair in 1893, "...even the new building for the display of this feathery tribe (the National Poultry Association had donated crops) proved to be inadequate for all who desired to compete."

The pens and crates were filled with fine strains. A trio of Wyandotte chickens belonging to W.A. Curtiss of Shirley took first premium in its grade that year, and the brown leghorn trio prize went to hens owned by W.E. Richmond. Two firsts for light Brahma chickens went to C.H. Ackerly of Gowanda. By 1897 the department drew 275 entries.

Unquestionably contributing largely to the interest in the department was an incubator owned by J.F. Norton of Eden Valley. In 1897 of 200 eggs, 95% were successfully hatched.

As new and better farm equipment and machinery called for "four to five times more space," in 1895 a building for the exhibition of Agricultural Implements and Machinery was ordered built. By 1897, "horse-powers, feed-cutters and windmills..." were in evidence.

Exhibits and premiums at the Fair in the 1890's merged the pioneer past of Western New York with the progressive vista of the approaching 20th century. A premium was offered in 1890 for "the best fifteen yards of woolen cloth make in the family." The prize was $10, which it was noted, " is as large as the premium offered for the best two acres of wheat."

By 1893 the "Cortland Home ventilating Stove," called "the furnace stove," made its debut. "It brings 1,500 cubic

feet of pure air into your room every hour," said the Commercial Advertiser, taking

out 600 and giving circulation that only varies from three to four degrees, heating from three to six rooms upstairs and down. It will do as much work as any two stoves."

Yet bees still hummed at the Fair. O.L. Hersheiren received $2 "for his exhibition of Bees and their products" and A. Graves of South Wales presented 41 varieties of grapes.

Society moved in 1892 to procure the necessary legislation to enable it to lease the grounds "for a summer meeting, or other legitimate purposes," and to use the rental for improvements.

By 1894, the issue apparently legalized, it was decided to rent the grounds "to responsible parties" to hold races on the 4th of July weekend, said party "to leave the track, grounds and buildings in as good condition as when they took them."

As the size and competitions at the Fair increased, rules were tightened.

A charge of $5 for the first horse and $2 for each additional horse was levied in 1893 "for the privilege of using the track, and the use of one stall for each horse, except during a regular fair. Monies to be paid in advance."

And restraining the overcompetitive, "no animal or article, after receiving a first premium shall compete for a premium in the same class and the same subdivision, until the expiration of two annual exhibitions thereafter. No person shall enter more than one animal or article to compete for the same."

Business was so brisk by 1892 that long time Marshall W.H. Knapp's salary was raised from $10.00 to $15.00, and he was provided an assistant at $10.00.

With swelling crowds, security too, was increased; Chief of police D.F. Prindle was raised to $20.00, and all police sported ribbon badges.

Pickpockets had long been a scourge at the Fair "no fewer than a dozen women reported their pockets had been picked…," complained the Buffalo Courier in 1895, "and the constables appeared to be afraid of the crooks." But by 1897, "Yesterday's crowd (not fewer than 15,000) would have been a test for a much larger and more experienced police force, yet there was no friction."

Publicity, the life-blood of any fair, was increased with advertisements being placed in local and city newspapers for three weeks prior to the Fair.

Gary Gardner was appointed to post bills and other advertising throughout the city of Buffalo, at $1.50 a day. And holding its head high, Society charged W. Beers of Titusville $20.00 "for the privileges of selling score cards, caps for drivers and numbers" at the Fair.

As the 19th century drew to a close, the

1890's

Commercial Advertiser gave Society a fine send off into the 20th, which would so revolutionize American farm life - indeed life in the United States and the World.

"The Association always pays its premiums which amounts to thousands of dollars, but sometimes they run very close to the cushion. This year (1897, the 41st Annual Erie County Fair) there will be plenty of money for all expenses and probably a good balance to apply top the debt of the Society, incurred by the purchase of additional ground about four years ago. The officers are delighted with the outlook."

End of 1890's

1890's

PART II
PLANTING

"Fairs bring us together...They render more pleasant, more strong, and more durable the bond of social and political union among us...

"Constituted as man is, he has positive need of occasional recreation. Such recreation our fairs afford...

"They make known to many, what was previously known to a few. They quicken the hand of genius...they stimulate discovery and invention into extraordinary activity."

Abraham Lincoln

Progress, therefore, is not an accident, but a necessity... It is part of nature.

Herbert Spencer

An Exposition all Its Own
Chapter 7

Small bells can ring in great events.

In the neighboring City of Buffalo in 1896 – now the largest rail center and agricultural storage area in the world – the clang-clang-clang of a trolley cruising up its Main Street foretold the power that would revolutionize "every middle-sex, village and farm" of Erie County. Electricity, that flashing mystery that would change the life of the area – from the lamp on the parlor table to transportation, from the tillage of soil to the milking of cows – had arrived at the gate of the Erie County Agricultural Society. Electricity celebrated itself as the radiant beams of the Electric Tower, centerpiece of the Pan-American Exposition, which Buffalo raised to show the world its maturity, industrially and culturally in 1901.

The beam brought people from around the world – 6,000,000 of them – and despite the horrific tragedy at the site of the great extravaganza, it not only brought the world to Erie County, but the county to the world.

Pictured above are the first trolley cars in the Town of Hamburg in Erie County. Opening of the line.

1900's

Yet Society, hardy, proud and on the move, was not over-awed by the Exposition. In 1964 it too would add the title "Exposition" to its original one of the "Erie County Fair," and also would receive crowds of hundreds of thousands.

Perhaps more pertinent to this growing agricultural display was the 1896 trolley clang, the Buffalo Hamburg and Aurora Railway - 15 miles of trolley line from Buffalo to Orchard Park and Hamburg.

Noted the Buffalo Courier-Express on October 6: "The Buffalo terminal is at the Seneca Street City Line, just beyond which are three sharp curves which need close watching. For a first trip, the Buffalo, Hamburg and Aurora Co. is to be congratulated on the success achieved yesterday"

"With the Stars and Stripes streaming from front and rear, that start was made by the two special cars at 1:35 p.m. Proceeding carefully over the new roadbed, Hamburg was reached at 2:33 p.m. -- without a hitch, barring a slight derailment at the second car near the village where some men were at work on the tracks. It took only 5 minutes to get 'agoing'.

"The incidents of the trip included many quaint spectacles of humanity en route. Teamsters in the field stopped work to stare in open-mouthed wonder at the horseless vehicle propelled, it seemed to them, by some uncanny power."

There were the fleeing hens scampering to a place of refuge from an imaginary foe; there was the farmers' howling dog that thought by racing and yelping along-side to stop the progress of the car." "It was reserved for a flock of geese to accomplish the feat. They had started onto the track, and seeing their danger, the motorman slowed up to give them time to wobble away."

"The scenery along the route of Buffalo, Hamburg and Aurora road is that of a picturesque, enormously fertile country, with water and woodland, abundance of orchards and pasture lands well-stocked with cattle." Speed was increased at Mile Strip when the car sped at a merry 20 miles-an-hour clip, and passed farmhouses whose occupants, young and old, came out and cheered lustily."

"William Abbott of Armor displayed a huge American flag in front of his homestead. His neighbor, Mr. Laub, gave forth a shriek of welcome from a steam whistle. The motorman responded with the clanging of the bell..."

"The townsfolk of Hamburg turned out en masse. Every porch was dotted with people. To clinch the welcome, a loud-mouthed cannon belched forth murderous notes in front of Kopp's Hotel."

"Landlord Kopp had his opera house (an entertainment hall) gaily decorated with flags, bunting and potted plants. Three long rows of tables occupied the auditorium. They were laden with the delicacies of the season, which were dished out by Proprietor Kopp in a manner to uphold the reputation of his hostelry."

"The first regular car (of 16) will leave Hamburg for Buffalo this morning at 6:40 o'clock. Six round trips will be made during the day, the last one reaching Hamburg at 10:23 p. "Whether unconsciously spurred on by the forceful imagery of the great Pan-American or propelled forward by its own vigorous momentum, Society became an institution in its own right in the first years of the 20th Century." Confidence, boldness and imagination drove together on the

highway that would lead the Erie County Fair and Exposition to the destination it occupies today – the second largest county fair in the United States.

Yet a distinctly rural aura pervaded the fair during the morning hours in 1900:

"The grounds were occupied chiefly by country people," reported the Commercial Advertiser, "most of whom were sitting about quietly visiting."   "The annual fair brings together a great many who never met at other places, and the renewing of old friendships is always one of the features of the first days."

"Shortly before noon, most of the visitors (who had left their farms at daybreak) withdrew to the adjoining woods and ate their lunches, coming back to the grounds ready and anxious for the races on the track, in magnificent condition, just enough rain having fallen to make it hard and smooth."

Buffalo visitors arrived a bit later in overflowing trains, with passengers standing in the aisles.

"The buses plying down between the station and the fairgrounds were taxed to their utmost capacity all day," noted the press. "With three and four horses attached to the big wagons, large loads of passengers could be carried, but hundreds of sightseers tired of waiting for rooms in the buses walked to the grounds."

As the day wore on, "it would have been hard to imagine a more cosmopolitan crowd." Country people and city people, businessmen and farmers, ladies in silk and women in calico, Indians and white men, 'mingling indiscriminately and enjoying themselves equally'."

Harbinger of a new age and future rival of those three and four-horse-team-buses, an automobile made rapid runs around the track to the amazement of country dwellers, whose life it would soon radically change.

Troupes of trapezists, acrobats and tumblers also relived inter-race tedium. Lay's Seneca Indian Band of Versailles, the Gowanda Band and the 74th Regiment Band of Buffalo played on with such hits as "On the Banks of the Wabash Far Away"…"Goodbye Dolly Gray," and "Stars and Stripes Forever."

Among the highlights of the land were the Agricultural Department's display of C. Nichols of Aurora of a plate of Japanese plums, which ripened in July and had been kept on ice "almost perfectly round in shape, golden in color and of delicious flavor,"

and some clusters of grapes from W.S. Clark of Eden Center "almost as large as plums." Merritt Bunting of Aurora showed 160 varieties of potatoes. Composed of blue and white asters, figures of a Dutch windmill and a battleship drew great attention in Floral Hall of the Women's Department where entries topped 2,500.

BUFFALO THE **ILLUSTRATED** **EXPRESS.**

PART 1.—PAGES 1 TO 12. BUFFALO, N. Y., SUNDAY, SEPTEMBER 24, 1905. PRICE FIVE CENTS.

And for "seasoning" about the grounds; the usual sideshows – the merry-go-round, "Hit-the-Baby and Get-a-Cigar," alleys for throwing rings over canes, tents where for 5 cents one could see calves and other animals "with any desired number of legs," etc…"

This was the Erie County Fair and Exposition as the century opened. On the general scene, "there has been no lack of confidence on the part of the Officers of the Fair Association," commented the Buffalo Evening News in 1901, "and much money has been expended in putting the grounds in first class condition." "New buildings for exhibits have been erected and the paintbrush had traveled over the buildings put up in years past, until the grounds were better equipped and more handsome than ever before."

A new grandstand replaced the original built in 1884. "The horse interest has revived," reported the Buffalo Times in 1901. "A very nice line of horses, matched and single brood mares and colts of all ages are shown."

Increased purses attracted a better class of horses to the races than ever before.

"Erie County produces many of the finest cattle in the world, many of which are shown," noted the Buffalo Times. A herd of fat cattle entered by Harry Brocksopp of Hamburg stood out. As to hogs, "of which there is nothing more profitable on the farm," they were there – big hogs, little hogs and pigs.

Camaraderie was an important by-product of the Fair. "The one thing that brings the busy, bustling citizens of Buffalo… and other parts of Erie County into close sympathy, and makes them of one mind on subjects that would otherwise find them far apart, is the Hamburg Fair," said the Buffalo Courier. "Its saving effect in healing old sores has proved with each recurring fair to be as efficacious as the balm of Gilead."

This amiability was particularly strong on Politicians Day, one of specially designated days at the Fair. There were two sides to the coin:

The Buffalo Evening News in 1903: "The Fair is a recognized stamping ground for county politicians and everybody who expects any favors from county delegates must be at the Fair with an extended hand and glad smile."

The Buffalo Courier: "Every office holder in Erie County, actual or expectant, will doubtless find his way to Hamburg…It is an open secret that a large number have been practicing the pump handle handshake and amassing a working farm knowledge for use on this occasion."

The stature of the Fair assumed was reflected in the prominence of speakers it drew to its rostrum.

The Hon. Charles R. Skinner, New York State Superintendent of Schools, made a special plea to parents of schools "to improve the general surroundings of school buildings" on Educational Day 1903. He urged they encourage the study of flowers and agriculture in order to cause children "to stick to farm life," which he considered the best

life for one to lead, reported the press.

Dr. John W. Spencer, professor of nature study at Cornell University, also spoke.

Amelia Cook, pupil of one-teacher school in Marilla, went home with a first prize for a map of North America.

Gov. Odell Watching the Stock Parade at the Hamburg Fair.

September 11, 1903, was proud day for the Fair. It was Governor's Day and Governor Benjamin B. Odell, Jr., dapper in top hat, addressed 18,000 there.

Society had done itself proud in presenting the grounds at their best, roads being oiled to keep the dust down: the old entrance replaced by one of modern design; ticket booths installed. A 100-foot Machinery Hall was erected for the increasing number of implements and laborsaving devices for the farmer in field and barn.

The sideshows were eliminated and replaced by driveways lined with flowerbeds.

"The flower of youth and beauty of Erie County was there," said the Buffalo Courier at the scene. "The young man with his best girl, the well-to-do farmer with his honest housewife and members of his family — all bedecked for the occasion, drove in rigs of every conceivable sort, from a buggy for two to a wagon for two dozen."

Many sat for tintypes, which would look out of albums decades

later in nostalgic quaintness.

In his speech, Governor Odell urged the necessity of maintaining the commercial prestige of the Empire State and enlargement of the Erie Canal.

Emphasizing the Fair's growing importance was the special car full of newspapermen brought to the grounds by J.B. Rumsey, general manager of the Buffalo and Southwestern Railroad. They were feted at luncheon in George J. Kopp's Hamburg Hotel.

The Erie County Fair celebrated its 50th birthday in 1906, by extending its run for the first time to six days.

Widening of the Fair's attraction too, was registered in the racing card's inclusion of entries from other localities throughout the State, as well as Indians and Ontario, and by the engagement of an out-of-towner, Mrs. P.S. Aldrich of Palmyra, N.J., as judge of the Women's Department.

Overall entries increased by a third, horses nearly one half.

The influence of the Pan-American had filtered down into the Fair's midway, which the Buffalo Courier assured readers "lacked nothing of the former's spaciousness and picturequeness."

"Weird strains from the Oriental dance exhibitions mingled with the spirited strains of the 74th Regiment Band."

The semi-centennial's Buffalo Day, the politicians' Mecca, drew all the candidates for county offices, and supervisors and former supervisors were "as common as send flies in August."

"The politicians failed to watch the horse race or baseball game, being too busy watching each other," slyly noted the Buffalo Times.

However, nobody seemed to enjoy themselves more than the 80 little children from the Indian Orphanage.

As the domestic barnyard and field life of Society ploughed on in 1908:

J.C. Newton was elected a committee of one to sell all the manure on (the) grounds; the pulling of stumps (persistent memorabilia of pioneer days) was assigned to the Grounds Committee; Albert Sawers won the contract for hay at $12.00 (a ton) and straw, $8.00

Society ruled all beggars be excluded from the grounds; single admission as set at 25 cents, men's membership, $1.00, ladies, 50 cents and a life membership was extended to R. W. Hengerer, "in

appreciation of his generous gift of a strip of land leading from Fair ground to the B. & S. R.R."

As the gate continued to increase, benches were ordered to be built and distributed throughout the Grove; a dog show was inaugurated under the supervision of John T. Roberts.

A $25.00 reward was offered for information leading to any person selling liquor on the grounds in 1909; H.B. Saunders hired a press agent, salary $50.00, and Miss Marian Moore awarded $1.50 for a duck she lost at the Fair.

End of 1900's

Working for Unity
Chapter 8

*The horse, the horse! The symbol of
surging Potency and power of movement
of action, in man.*

David Herbert Lawrence

Society smashed all records on Buffalo Day 1910, at the Erie County Fair and Exposition, with a gate of 20,000.

Special arrangements with four rail services, the Buffalo & Susquehanna, the Buffalo Southern, the Erie and the International Railway Co., and cars of the Buffalo & Lake Erie Transaction Co. now brought Buffalonians to the grounds to join the farms' population, who made the event possible.

Grounds where "every fence and building were painted, lawns cut, flowers and shrubbery planted and new benches scattered around the shade of the tall pines," described the press.

But the railroads were not alone, the automobile was beginning to claim the countryside.

"The largest number of automobiles ever gathered at the annual fair stood within the enclosure of the race track...," reported the Buffalo Times, "fully 700 machines pass through the gate during the day.

1910's

COUNTY FAIR

1910's

"The scene inside the grounds was of indescribable beauty, the vari-colored gowns of the women as they lined the length of the race course, both inside and outside the rail, mingling in the splendid harmony with the gaily festooned grandstand and the well-decorated exhibits."

Backed by the two great breeding establishments which made East Aurora, N.Y. famous, the Jewett and Hamlin farms, the three-day race meet brought on "the greatest field of harness horses ever brought together on a county fair grounds," according to the Buffalo Evening News.

"Eighty-four stalls are provided for race horses…," noted the Buffalo Courier, "and last night every one was filled. Never before in the history of the Fair have the various events been filled so completely…"

Purses were as high as $500.

The highlight of the horse show in 1910 was the exhibit of registered Shetland ponies by Mrs. H.L. Allen of Alden.

"The string of ten, headed by the coal black stallion, Ancestor, only 12 inches high, imported from England by Mrs. Allen, made beautiful sight when shown together," said the Buffalo Courier. "A pair of yearling Shetlands were shown by this stable, the two making the smallest pair of horses ever seen at the County Fair."

Perhaps star of the track was "Amos R.," known as the "Guideless Wonder," owned by S.D. Cronk of Buffalo. A wonderfully trained horse, he circled the runway at top speed without rider or driver.

Additional tents were ordered from Buffalo to accommodate the many head of cattle, sheep and swine that arrived on opening day.

1910's

The Society for the Prevention of Cruelty to Animals made its debut at the 1910 Fair. They furnished a large sup-ply of drinking pails for dogs and horses, which were placed about the grounds. Literature on the subject of kindness to animals was given out in a rest tent for visitors.

Increasingly Society realized that its public, particularly its rural one, sought entertainment as well as husbandry. Three daily performances on an open air stage by comedians and acrobats were featured, headlining "Daredevil Dave," who climbed a 135-foot pole to dive into a tank containing 12 feet of water; also a performer on skates, rolling down a 100-foot incline turning a double somersault
into a water-filled tank. Such sights pleased country folk.

A gate prize of $50.00 was awarded two days of the fair to encourage attendance.

One cloud shadowed the horizon. The first day of the 1910 Fair (an institution that had long held liquor on its grounds at bay and opened its platform to the WTCU) a saloon opened in a tent on the main road, in a field a little over 600 feet from the grounds.

One Gustavas A. Krause had obtained a license to do so for the second year. Society, caught unaware, had not resisted the first operation.

"As the business was carried on last year the place was surrounded by the worst characters from Buffalo," reported the Buffalo Express. "The people generally who patronize the fair are very indignant that liquor should be sold there in that way."

Society acted swiftly, telephoning State Excise Commissioner Clement for a special agent to investigate the case and revoke the license.

Two agents arrived but said they could not legally remove it.

"Right on top of this," described the Express, "half a dozen gambling outfits were established under some big oak trees across the street from where the beer and other liquors were sold…"

The last report was that Society was "making a hard fight" to have Barkeep Krause's license revoked; the outcome is not recorded.

"See 'Em – these female jockeys at the Erie County Fair" exclaimed the Buffalo Times on September 15, 1915, as they thundered around the track.

"Here are ye suffragettes… 'lady jockeys' are racing every afternoon. They made a big hit yesterday and will appear every matinee."

"These particular 'jockeys' are not so very skinny as some we've seen at Fort Erie. In fact they might make good candidates for a fat ladies race or something like that, but what's the use 'o'kickin' about their weight. The race is the thing!" Suffragettes were delighted.

Despite the growing popularity of the race track, games and entertainment, "the primary object of the Erie County Agricultural Society in giving the fair this year," reported the Buffalo Express, "was to promote agricultural interests, to bring out the advantage of Erie County for remunerative farming and to encourage school work in the county districts."

Yet mechanization of farm and rural life was here to stay, and despite the 4,000 entries in the Poultry Department doubling any previous year, an automobile show displaying all well known makes was substituted for the usual livestock show that was cancelled due to the recent outbreak of hoof-and-mouth disease. Cars "particularly best adapted to the use of farmers" were featured.

All kinds of mechanical devices for making the farmer's work easier and more productive – "from the latest electric churners to the big complicated Reuther potato diggers" also were shown.

"The display of farming machinery contains many motor-drawn implements unknown to the agricultural world of a generation age," commented the Buffalo Courier.

Supervisors of the five educational districts in the county conducted the Educational Exhibit. Every county school whose pupils were exhibiting was closed on Children's Day.

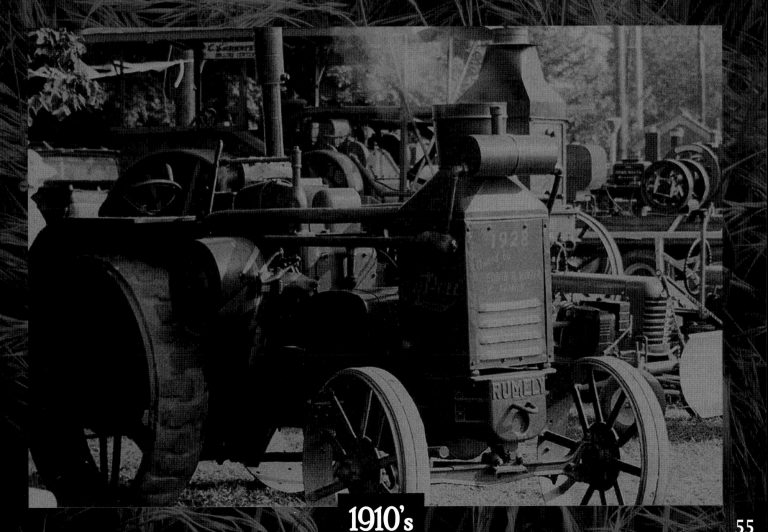

1910's

Bazaar Hall was the site of exhibits of nine Granges, representing Eden, Collins Center, Evans Center, Wales Center, East Aurora, Boston, Orchard Park, Hamburg and Lawtons. A $50.00 cup was given as a special premium in the Grange section at the 1916 Fair.

There were specialties: Prof. A.E. Wilkinson of Cornell University headed the New York State Agricultural exhibit. Vegetables raised by the university's students were displayed.

Advocates of the suffrage "invaded" the grounds to hear well-known speakers from across the state and boost their cause.

President R.W. Hengerer tried to be fair, also giving space to the Buffalo Branch of the New York Association Opposing Suffrage the next day. "We believe Erie County people want to hear both sides of the question," he said.

"In and out among the 20,000 visitors, they (the suffragettes) worked their way, and few were political leaders who escaped," reported the Buffalo Evening News. "One by one, they were run down and cornered with a request to sign a suffrage petition. A few signed at once. Many protested feebly, but in the end they also signed."

Then the beaming suffragette would pin an artificial daisy and a "Votes for Women" badge on the blushing politician and collect a dime.

Anti-suffragette Margaret C. Uhl said that even if women did get the franchise it would have little if any effect because "80 percent of women votes being married, they would only nullify or double their husbands votes."

But the suffragettes appeared a second day beyond their allotted time.

"We are in politics now and cannot wait to be asked as if we were going to an afternoon tea," said Mrs. Frank J. Shuler, campaign chairman in Western New York.

The Women's Department headed by Mrs. N.G. Parker continued to soar with 3,000 entries, including exhibits of fancywork such as "articles of embroidery in French jeweled, cross-stitch, honiton, Oriental and Bulgarian, Mount Mellick, coronation outlining, eyelet, darned and punch work."

A "Novelty and Sales Department" was opened in which exhibitors could show small articles, that following inspection by the judges, could be sold. A Children's and Older Woman's exhibit was also started.

On a more aesthetic level, Dr. Cornelius B. sage, director of the Albright Art Gallery, in awarding a first prize to J.J. Lankes of Buffalo's portrait of a woman, commented that "there were hundreds of art works at the fair that would not be out of place in any exhibition of high-class work of this character."

But field, barn and coop came through: 3 pound cucumbers, 2 feet long; 15 pound pumpkins; green corn hanging from stalks 12 feet tall or more; eggplants as large as a good-sized watermelon.

There were 143 kinds of apples, 32 varieties of peaches, 55 of pears and 57 of choice plums.

"The horticultural display contains many entries that bear evidence front porches have been robbed of their verdure," noted the Buffalo Courier. "There are immense ferns that could not have obtained their magnificent growth without the kindly attention of devoted hands."

When it came to the 4,000-entry poultry section the Buffalo Evening News remarked with tongue in cheek:

"One does not have to be very well versed in chicken language to gather the impression that, when a lot of feathered hens get together the talk they indulge in is not unlike that one hears when a lot of _____" (here the paper lost its nerve).

"The exhibit ranges in size from tiny varieties that one could tuck away in his inside pockets, to monster specimens that a whole family couldn't eat in a week..."

Blue ribbons went to a pair of Sebastapol geese, imported by P.E. Nulling of Woodville, N.Y. Also shown was a duck, said to be "the smallest bird of the duck family in the world."

But as it would be in the future, racing and entertainment continued as big factors in the success of the Erie County Fair. The farmer who has plowed and

1910's

the city resident, always searching for excitement, responded enthusiastically and generously to these two features.

"A greater variety of amusements than management ever has undertaken before," reported the Buffalo Times of the 59th Fair in 1915. Some of the fastest pacers in the country were entered in the trotting races.

Two particular listings were a half-mile run around the track by two teams of dapple gray fire horses attached to heavy hose wagons trimmed in burnished brass, gongs sounding at intervals of a second. "The perfect condition of the horses was demonstrated by the fact that they were scarcely 'blowing' at the end of the run," remarked the Buffalo Evening News. And brewery horses, heavy draft type, now were in the Horse Show, a member of the Buffalo brewers having entered their finest.

An exhibition of jumping and leaping horses listed a blind horse heralded as "the most talented horse in the world," and another acclaimed as "the tallest" jumping one.

Bonnie Cope, a bay mare from Virginia, was first in the 2.14 pace race for a $400 purse.
There were motorcycle races on a sugar bowl track.

1910's

The Midway had been extended 100 yards longer on both sides of the road - a forecast of future expansion.

A Fat Lady beamed on her public, and in an adjoining tent the Thin Man "dressed in an umbrella cover, grows more like a fountain pen each year."

Apale's Animal Circus performed. There was free vaudeville every afternoon in front of the grandstand, where Hyers Orchestra played all day. Tunes of the times were "Alexander's Ragtime Band"; "Sweet Mystery of Life" and "I want a Girl Just Like the Girl that Married Dear Old Dad…"

Indicative of changing times and the interest of city dwellers in gardening was the fact that Buffalo exhibitors figured more conspicuously in 1915 as prize winners than ever before. For example, tomatoes raised within the city limits captured blue ribbons in competition with experienced farmers.

But "city folk" still represented "the glass of fashion" to country ones at the Fair:

"Those who come from farms and villages," noted the Buffalo Courier, "will furtively gaze with a mixture of astonishment and admiration at those of the city who flaunt their sartorial effects."

Yet city and country were getting closer:

"In order to help handle the crowds – now running as high as 20,000 a day – the Buffalo & Southern Railroad built a spur which will run directly to the fairgrounds," reported the Buffalo Morning Express.

End of 1910's

1910's

A Busy-a-Fair
Chapter 9

You can plan a Fair to the last detail but human – correction, animal nature – and the weather can slow things up considerably.

"There will be a greater variety of agricultural livestock and handiwork exhibits this year than ever before in the history of the Fair," announced the Buffalo Express in 1920.

Three times as many exhibits and such large crowds that were obliged to walk in single line to view them.

A new aviation field of 25 acres was opened. A 10-acre field was set aside for auto parking.

The horse show was the largest ever.

And, for the first time in its history, the Erie County Fair, owing to bad weather, was open on Sunday.

The star performers at the opening day of the Fair, however, neither flew, ran nor trotted. They were respectively, a prize-winning Holstein Bull and a 1,000 pound hog.

"The bull was a bit peevish to start with, what with being dragged from the old pasture, hustled into an auto truck and dumped out with scant ceremony…," reported the Express. "But after they had finished putting the ring through his nose – he was one mad bull. All they needed was a toreador to have a bullfight… They finally got him into a stall with bars on the front large enough to hold an elephant, by the expedient of hooking a bullpole through the ring and backing him in."

1910's

Then there was the farmer and his mammoth hog that didn't want to leave the crate that had come to seem like the old homestead to him.

"Bristles, straw and debris flew in all directions as the farmer swore and punched and the hog squealed and clung to the crate," explained the Express.

"Gol rum yuh! I'll fix yuh!" yelled the farmer, who then mustered the services of onlookers and backed his truck up against the side of the pen, where all hands tipped the crate and cascaded the pig into it; he immediately dined on the choice swill.

After the opening incidents, the Erie County Fair progressed.

An honored guest was Mrs. Silas Potter of Armor, age 90, who had attended all 63 of the previous fairs.

But the balance between old and new, tradition and progress was visibly emerging at the Erie County Fair. The novelty of certain key events and the public's reaction to them testified to the distance the Fair had come.

Take Children's Day in 1920. Supervisor Frank A. Dorn issued a call for 500 autos to take about 20,000 boys and girls of school age from Buffalo and towns of the county to the Fair. Unquestionably many of these youngsters had not traveled by auto before. Unfortunately, rain cancelled the plan.

But there were so many autos entered in the Motor Show that tents had to be erected outside the building to accommodate them.

Then there was the air activity; "Edwin N. Ronne, aviator from the Buffalo Curtiss field, is the pilot of the plane that is taking passengers into the air," reported the Buffalo Evening News. "This afternoon, he took President C.J. Dudley and Secretary Charles H. Fosdick for a circling tour above the fairgrounds, giving them a bird's eye view of Hamburg and the towns for miles around. He flew at a height of about 5,000 feet.

"Great Stuff!" commented both officials enthusiastically when they stepped back on old terra farms.

"The next passenger was Supervisor Charles Bogold, who tips the scales at 210 pounds. He was so wide of girth that the safety strap would not go around him, so he considered to go up without it."

Mrs. Potter must have smiled and shaken her head, as Fair memories merged with the reality of the flight.

And Society was very proud.

"The World War has taught citizens of both the city and the country that they are dependent, each on the other," declared Acting Mayor Arthur Kreinheder, known as the silver-tongued orator of Chautauqua, at the 1920 Fair. Frank H. Mott, Democratic candidate for Attorney General, also spoke.

"The League of Nations is the big issue in the campaign and the enemies of President Wilson are enemies of the league too," he said. "These anti-league obstructionists do not hesitate to pervert the real aim of the league and the real objects of the various league covenants."

Sitting on the sidelines in amazement were Samuel K. Willett of Mile Strip Road, Hamburg, and Zeb Sly of Orchard Park. Mr. Willett, age 91, attended the first annual Fair formally organized by Society, which was held on Indian Church Road in 1856. Mr. Sly, also in his 90's, hadn't missed one for 51 years.

"About two weeks before the (1856) fair," remembers Mr. Willett, "I was visited by George Pierce, the first president of the Society. He asked me to send my men and a team of oxen to help uproot stumps on the grounds in Indian Church Road. We were all willing to pitch in to make the fair a success... "The first trotting races were held at the fair sixty-eight years ago. I had a lively pony that I used to draw the milk wagon. When I was asked to enter him in the trotting races, I refused at first, saying the pony didn't know the difference between a racetrack and a bootblack. But I entered him anyway, and he won. Racing became a popular feature after that."

Lewis H. Willett, Society president, was a cousin of Samuel.

"The real meaning of the league means the adoption of a practical plan whereby security of all and freedom of each of the nations shall be obtained."

National Democratic Committeeman Norman E. Mack escorted Mr. Mott to the Fair.

Only "a clean variety" of shows were staged in the enlarged midway.

More than 15 Granges exhibited.

As the Fair matured it took on a more "landed gentry" air. Fine horse flesh has long been an accompaniment of wealth and fashion, including race, draft and driving animals, and the more than 350 horses at the Fair as the 20's opened, struck a prestigious note in the agricultural spectacle.

The pick of the stables of such prominent Western New Yorkers as George P. Urban, Mr. & Mrs. Howard Kellogg, Col. W.J. Donovan, J.P. Schoellkopf and William A. Morgan were among those exhibited.

A Mrs. Devine of Monroe, Wis., brought in 16 Shetland Ponies to the Fair, as entertainment for the children.

But the press did not wax entirely elitist before this entire stylish turnout: "Six of its finest horses were entered by the Buffalo Street Department," noted the Buffalo Evening News finest horses were entered by the Buffalo Street Department," noted the Buffalo Evening News with proletarian candor.

Among leading exhibitors of cattle were Harry Yates of Orchard Park; Oliver Cabana Jr., Buffalo; Clark H. Burd, Elma; and W. Machenes of Eden. Artists exhibiting included Clara Langenbach, Evelyn Rumsey, Robert North, E.L. Sprague and Frank A. Ford. On the opening race day, Fred Jones, owned by R.F. Dygert of Springville, won the John N. Brandy Futurity of the Buffalo Road Drivers.

The United State was riding high in the saddle in 1925. And so was the Erie County Fair & Exposition.

"With by far the largest and most interesting exhibition entry list that has ever graced a county fair program, with interest in city and county areas running at a pitch never before attained, the outlook for the 69th exposition is admittedly very bright," heralded the Buffalo Courier as the Fair opened.

A harbinger of things to come was the growing interest in the Conservation Building, where fish, live and mounted, were on display, augmented by a new outdoor aquarium. Pike, bass, sturgeon, sunfish and other fish found in the county's waters were shown.

County Rod & Gun Clubs also exhibited. The Fair had an unprecedented range and variety. It seemed to have come into full flower. Every department — from bursting cattle sheds to stylish horse show ring, from premium winners broadcast by Station WEBR each afternoon, to an embracing press — shone.

The strong, pleased faces of "The Men Behind the 69th Fair" on the front page of the Buffalo Express, some of whose forebearers had founded the fair, testified to its success. A six-day Fair featured on Opening Day, Children's Day, Conservation Day, Buffalo or Politician's Day and Western New York Day.

Animals were the star performers either in show ring or on track.

"It has been said that Western New York cattle are famed from one end of the country to the other," noted the Buffalo Courier of the 300-400 size herds exhibited under Superintendents Clark Hurd and Charles H. Brown. Many arrived by railroad car.

Superstar of the lot, which included Shorthorns, Durhams, Anguses, Galloways and Brown Swiss, was Holstein bull Daul Seges Posch Overbrook, tipping the scales at 2,400 pounds.

William H. Knapp, horseshow chairman, announced 621 entries, some from as far west as the Mississippi, as well as Canada. There were 25 events a day, showing from ponies of less than 42 inches high to draft horses weighing around a ton — Belgian, Hackney, Percheron, Saddle, Shetlands and thoroughbred breeds.

"In the tandem class for Shetlands, three pairs made a beautiful exhibition," reported the Buffalo Evening News. "The draft horses, shown in teams of three (15 chestnuts and 15 grays) by the Bureau of Streets of the Department of Public Works...one of the finest sights seen in the show ring."

Two especially interesting entries were

"Kilmahan," owned by E.L. Woodward, and Yates Farms' "You'll Do," who fought a sprinted battle but lost to "Kilmahan."

The Gentleman's Appointment Class for harness horses included two mares, "Queen Mary" and "Queen Elizabeth," both owned by Charles G. Duffy of Buffalo. Contrary to history, in competition Mary beat out Elizabeth.

Horse show and trotting entry fees were estimated at about $250,000; horse show premiums, $10,000 and purses for the trotting races "the largest of any county fair of the state," according to the Buffalo Express. The Buffalo Road Drivers stake for the 2.20 trot was $1,100 alone.

There was a half-mile race for polo ponies – an indication of how "fashionable" the horse show had become – but the most ambitious act was the chariot race:

"Glories of ancient Rome were recalled at the Erie County Fair…," breathlessly reported the Buffalo Courier. "Sgt. Melvin Sunders and Sgt. Frank Trautman of Troop E., Buffalo, wearing glittering steel helmets and coats of mail, with flowing cloaks…stood erect in bespangled chariots (with four horses each) and sped around the half-mile track grandiloquently."

The "Four Hundred of Dogdom," as the press put it, was present at the Buffalo Kennel Club Show at the Fair. There were 500 entries of 40 breeds. The star of this galaxy was World's Champion "Choonun Brilliantine," a $10,000 Chow Chow entered by Mrs. H. Earl Hoover of Glencoe, Ill., who looked with lofty mien at the crowds admiring his dignity and glowing russet coat.

An exhibition of three Doberman pinschers, trained for police work, was given by police officers, included were criminal tracking, ladder-climbing, fence-jumping and obedience stunts. The chief performer was "Dobber Von Dorasheim," who was credited with jumping a distance of "nine feet, nine inches over a stone wall with no start."

How to cull (choose the best) hens and select breeding stock was demonstrated by a representative of the Poultry Department at Cornell University at the Farm Bureau booth in the Grange Hall.

Harbinger of the future was "an educational table" sponsored by the Erie County League of Women Voters in the Women's Department. It stood side by side with 18 sections of handicrafts for the home and wearing apparel, and antiques and articles made by hospital and institution patients.

Imagine the reaction to such material by the woman who stitched the 200-year-old sampler exhibited by Mrs. Gladys A. Swift of Hamburg that won first prize!

Work by Indians on the reservations of grass and reed, beadwork pieces and woodcarvings was also shown. Indians had just been given the right to vote in the United States.

A growing consciousness of health and childcare was reflected at the Society for the Prevention and Control of Tuberculosis station, "where children will be weighed and instruction given to parents as to how to increase the weight of children, who are below normal." And the Red Cross offered a center staffed by nurses where mothers could park their offspring while viewing the Fair.

Two bands played on either side of the Midway, the tunes of the day – "Barney Google," "Yes, We Have No Bananas" and "I wonder What's Become of Sally"… A harmonica contest open to all children of the count offered lively competition.

What would a fair be without the sideshow tent to satisfy the curiosity of the public in beyond the "norm"? It was still there – "The Plump Snake Charmer, Copper-Throated Fire-eater and Tinseled Palm-Reader make fond bids for nimble dimes" as the Buffalo Courier put it.

But over the memories, the nostalgia and the tradition signs of a "new" world were seen and heard. There were 10,000 parking spaces reserved at the 69th Erie County Fair in 1926, on Politician's Day. And each afternoon across track, barn and pen, the voice of radio station WEBR broadcast the result of races and livestock class winners.

In a decade when Capt. Charles A. Lindbergh flew over the Atlantic in 33 ½ hours, much was afoot.

End 1920's

Man, unlike any other thing, organic or inorganic in the universe, grows beyond his work, walks up the stairs of his concepts, emerges ahead of his accomplishments.

John Steinbeck

The Old and the New
Chapter 10

Standing squarely on its new 136 acres, the Erie County Agricultural Society opened its 74th Fair with the erection of a handsome new main gate on McKinley Parkway. The 40-foot span allowed four automobiles to enter abreast.

The approach to the Fair in 1930 on well-paved roads, with so impressive an entrance, was a long way from the dust-clouded highways to a simple plank that had led county farmers and their herds and flocks to the Fair on its 12 and two one hundredth acres stand nearly 50 years before.

Several new barns for mounting livestock entries, pavilions and a new row of boxes to accommodate the rising numbers of ringside spectators had been built.

All departments had record entries.

Signpost of a "new age" was the Buffalo Evening News report: "the automobile races on Saturday will be a novel attraction. There will be eight races, under license from the American Automobile Association and this program, with the exception of free attractions, will take up the entire afternoon."

1930's

And perhaps most glorious of a11, was the fact that "this season, for the first time, the grandstand had been equipped with a specially built amplifying system... It consists of five dynamic speakers in the grandstand and a magnetic speaker near the horse stables, with a 55 watt output, said to be the most powerful employed."

A long shadow of the future appeared at the Fair in 1930. Instead of a pretty girl, a strange looking metal object passed out health rhymes at the exhibit of the Buffalo Tuberculosis Association. The infectious disease would be largely controlled in the future, but the strange object, which was called a "robot", would outlive it.

Battle competition and sport characterized other novelties at the Fair. Enactment of war seems to entertain even in times of peace. Two men from the 174th Regiment staged a sham battle in the oval in the center of the race track, involving a platoon of machine guns, one of howitzers and two of rifles; 6,000 rounds of ammunition lit up the scene.

Inspired by such military efforts, the American Legion Buffalo Fife and Drum Corps, winner of first prize at the Paris convention and the New York State Title, both in 1927, sent its stirring strains over the grounds under the direction of C.G. Koelin. National Champion baton twirler Lee Supple accompanied them.

Of course too, there was the battle between animal husbandry and the hunt.

"The Buffalo Museum of Science is one of the exhibitors at the Erie County Fair at Hamburg this week,"

1930's

reported the Buffalo Evening News. "The Conservation Building is the scene of the exhibit, which is intended to interest the man who hunts. Here the visitor will find a display of hunting weapons made mostly from Africa, where natives have only homemade tools to work with.

"Included in the exhibit are hunting spears, bows, arrows, shields, daggers, battle-axes and different types of guns … Some striking heads of animals complete the exhibition …"Last but not least, there was the perennial delight of bait and fly casting for the Erie County championship including the 5 ¾ rod wet fly accuracy test, the 5 ¾ rod dry fly accuracy event, and the fisherman's bait accuracy competition.

An intimation however, that America was beginning to realize that the forest primeval and its streams were not inexhaustible was the large exhibit of the Izaak Walton League, which "by means of pictures and signs, the dire lesson of game and forest prevention is driven home," noted in the media: "Preserve the great outdoors for future generations and you will have a finer America and better Americans."

The fight between horse and machine was dramatically portrayed by the pulling contest where "during recent years State and National records have been broken and world marks approached."

To return to the comparative peace of barn and pen, the livestock broke records in some classes at the 1930 Fair: 323 head of cattle, 50 to 60 breeds of poultry, and 350 rabbits.

Superstar of the swine coterie was the Poland China 3-year-old black-as-coal boar, owned by Marvin Way of Martinville, Pa., grand champion of three previous fairs that year.

The horses, a reputed 700 of them on the grounds, held center stage in amusement.

There was the night harness racing for which the Erie County Fair had become nationally famous.

1930's

The annual Buffalo Road Drivers $20,000 stake circuit, drawing high-class horses from all over the country." stated Al K. Standish of Boston, Mass.,he heralded as being one of America's foremost starters, officiated.

The horse show, which in addition to such important local stables as those of Albert E. Buyers, Mr. and Mrs. Langdon B. Wood, Mr. And Mrs. Howard Kellogg and Irvine J. Kittinger drew entries from such equestrian seats as the Richard K. Mellon tables of Pittsburgh, Pa.

"Quite ritzy was the Horse Show, with lines of swanky cars around the ring and a new pavilion with easy chairs and flower boxes," noted the press of the scene.

The Junior League served tea nearby.

Capping the modishness of the horse show were works by the noted animal painter George Ford

Morris, who displayed paintings of two mounts of Miss Greta V. Schoonmaker of Green Valley Stables at Sewickley, Pa., Bachelor's Hope, an Irish thoroughbred, and Picturesque, a saddle-bred mare.

Commented the press: "More than 30 years ago, Mr. Morris, then only 17 years old, made a portrait for Cicero J. Hamlin, local owner of

a distinguished breeding farm, of his famous trotting mare, Nightingale, then holder of a world's trotting record. This painting is considered one of the finest specimens of horse portraiture in existence.

"Among the works recently completed by Mr. Morris in his studios at Shrewsbury, NJ, and Aiken, S.C., are a series of eight paintings in pastel for Seymour H. Knox of Buffalo, including a portrait of his son Seymour, on his piebald Shetland pony, riding through the woods of the Knox place at Aiken, S.C."

But there also was democracy in the show ring. Farm or draft horses, great animals weighing 2,800 pounds or over, made a powerful spectacle driven three abreast. Even a class for the humble milk delivery horse of 1,400 pounds or over was included.

Society attributed at least a part of its Fair's success to the fact that its events and exhibits were open during its entire span.

"Other fairs take for granted two bad days, the first, or moving-in day, and the last, or tearing-up day," an official pointed out. "Erie County Fair managers long ago eliminated these handicaps

by deciding to have no first or last day. The fair has to be there when it opens…and when taps are sounded on the last night."

Children's Day continued to grow in importance. Nearly 15,000 boys and girls were admitted free to the 1930 Fair; the event both educated and entertained.

Reported the Buffalo Evening News:

"A full program has been arranged…including admission to the grandstand attractions, a parade in which they participate around the race track and sports and athletic events."

Of special interest to the boys and girls were their own exhibits. Samples of lessons and exercises done in all the schools in Erie County outside of Buffalo were presented, giving rural youth a more recognized place in the sun.

To such tuned as "Happy Days are here again" and "There's A Rainbow 'Round my Shoulder," 2,000 children paraded in costume. Scores exhibited their pets ranging from mongrel dogs to tame crows and parrots.

The Eden Children's band won a silver cup.

Children of Buffalo playgrounds offered dances and drills on the outdoor stage in front of the grandstand.

The wide variety of ethnic numbers included a Polish (Krakowiak) dance, Houghton playground; tap dance, Lincoln playground; Tarantalla, St. Anthony's School; Irish lilt, Wende Playground, and flag drill, German Roman Catholic Orphan Asylum.

The copy of Elbert Hubbard's "Message to Garcia" was presented to Frank Beauvais of the Thomas Indian School at Gowanda, the second Indian Eagle Boy Scout in the world.

An exhortation to all dairymen was made by the Farm Bureau to weed out "loafer" cows in their herds by administering the so-called Babcock test.

All the dairymen had to do was to take a monthly sample of the milk given by each of his cows and estimate the amount of feed she eats each day. Small bottles for milk samples and a mailing carton were provided by the Bureau, which would then reckon the monthly production of the particular cow in question and determine whether she was "a profit maker or a boarder."

1930's

Down in the cattle sheds, the Erie County Boys Calf and Baby Beef Clubs groomed such little beauties as 10 black and shining Aberdeen Angus beeves, while the Heifer Calf Club curried nine budding cows. A splendid training ground for future farmers.

Fifteen Home Bureau units competed in such varied projects as community meals, food preservation, dramatics, medicine cabinet supplies and veranda refreshments.

It was the old and the new at the Erie County Fair – as fairs should be. A set of wooden tools over 100 years old was shown in the Women's Department antique section, where Mrs. Walter A. Clark of Eden displayed the faded and tattered uniform of her great-great grandfather, Dr. William Hill, a surgeon during the Revolutionary War.

A more current medical note was the comment of the Buffalo Evening News on the leather and bronze fancywork made by inmates of the Gowanda State Hospital.

"The making of these articled, the newspaper noted, "is a form of therapeutics used in treatment of mental diseases at the hospital. It is said the many times a patient – his mind thus turned to new channels – has recovered his sanity."

William A. Shepard, 103, of West Seneca, fondly known as "Old Shep," was on hand.

"Good for a half-a-dozen more fairs too…," he said. "Goat's milk accounts for a long life."

Little Ann Rose Griffith, 5 was top for originality in the children's parade, wheeling three kittens in a baby carriage around the track.

Miss Ida Funmitz of Buffalo got a first for her embroidered card table cover and Mrs. J. Klein of the city, for a piano scarf.

"Yep, long hair is returning to favor," commented the press. "Rural high school girls (who had daringly bobbed theirs in the '20's) are trying to braid it and do it up in back. Some of them looked good."

Anyway – "Old Shep" would have thought so.

Farm Organization Day was a feature of the Erie County Fair in 1935. All leading agricultural organizations in the county demonstrated their purpose and their work. Clayton C. Taylor of Lewiston was Director.

Events of the day included horseshoe pitching and a softball game for County championships.

Floats illustrating important developments in the care and handling of milk in the past decade; contrast of the former care of milk on farms with that of today; past and present transportation; quality control and field service; laboratory control and value of milk.

The Erie County Farm Bureau depicted its growth over 15 years, and the 4-H Clubs demonstrated their expansion in homemaking, tree-planting and livestock growing.

Side by side in the Industrial Building, industrial, mercantile and automobile exhibits drew increased interest.

The Women's Department, now with an organization rivaling that of the Fair administration itself, offered $2,000 in premiums in 14 sections open to county residents. Every exhibitor of handiwork was required "to be the maker of the same and to have executed it within five years."

In 1929, the Great Depression had swept the land. More than 20,000 people were served Christmas dinner in 1931, in Erie County Soup Kitchens.

1930's

But as Scott Eberle and Joseph A. Grande note in their publication; "Second Looks, A Pictorial History of Buffalo and Erie County: "The prosperous Erie County farm community, with its access to the huge Buffalo (now a city of 573,076) market, did not suffer the worst effects of the Depression."

Despite falling prices in milk, crops and livestock, the farmers ran wholesale produce markets in town and sold directly to the

consumer. They also cooperated with the Farm Bureau. Undaunted, in 1932 the Fair scheduled its first six-day run.

Erie County and Buffalo were ready with plans for projects when President Roosevelt's "New Deal" launched its federal public works programs, the Public Works Administration (PWA) and the Works Project Administration (WPA).

Reported to the Courier Express on October 7, 1935: "Plans for new structures and other improvements at the County fairgrounds, as a major WPA project in Erie County, will be completed and filed with Francis J. Downing, WPA director this week…"

"Plans call for three new buildings, locations of which already have been selected. They are an addition to the Conservation Building, a new structure for Women's exhibits and one additional exhibition building."

"Other work includes the construction of an inner fence, the laying of sidewalks and the landscaping

1930's

of grounds."

Cost of the work was estimated at $120,000, of which the county would pay the cost of materials, approximately $20,000 (a later version was $75,000). WPA would pay the remaining $100,000 in labor.

Amusements continued to gain popularity as the years progressed. More than 12 special novelty shows animated the 1938 Fair.

There were the horse acts – the Stanley Equestrian Race and Specialty Organization's Chariot, Roman standing and flat races and jumping, and trained horses; also the famous Troop C Rough Riders of the New York State Police under the command of Captain Daniel E. Fox.

But the popularity of the risk and thrill engendered by the mechanized motion was increasingly evident. Horses had performed on battlefields and in the show ring for generations, but such acts as Lucky Teter and his Hell Drivers, automobile and motorcycle stunt artists "who do seemingly impossible stunts with automobiles and motorcycles" raised the rural, indeed citified, blood pressure, to an even higher pitch. Mr. Teter and cast were said to have wrecked more than 1,500 autos in their career.

Ira Veil, noted auto race promoter, presented some of the world's most famous drivers on the legitimate track.

Higher-toned fare was the Roxeyette Revue of New York City, presented by the noted showman George S. Hamid, on a stage opposite the grandstand.

Addressing the annual meeting of Society in 1939, Mr. Hamid complimented Erie County on its fine standing in the fair world.

The evening climaxed with fireworks featuring a dazzling reproduction of the historic Wells-Fargo Express train robbery.

And in stall and pen, the animals, used to the quiet of country nights, stirred in their sleep:

The Holstein Friesian, Jersey, Guernsey, Ayrshire, Brown Swiss, Hereford, and Aberdeen Angus cattle.

The Horned Dorset, Cheirot, Hampshire, Lincoln, Southdown, Shropshire, Rambouillet, Cotswold, and Oxford Downs sheep.

The Chester White, Poland China, Duroc Jersey and Berkshire swine.

And the Alpine, Nubian, Saanen and Toggenburg goats.

In 1939, the New York World's Fair opened in glory. But as world fairs came and were gone – The Erie County Agricultural Fair and Exposition, high in the saddle, rode on.

End of 1930's

The Tradition Continues
Chapter 11

The Erie County Agricultural Society was 100 years old in 1940. Its origin, of course, dated back to 1819, when it was part of the Niagara County Horticultural Society, a span of 121 years. But the Society heralds its official start as 1841, with its reorganization as a continuous body dedicated to "the promotion of the Educational, Horticultural, Mechanical and Manufacturing interests" of Erie County.

Society celebrated its Centennial with fervor. Centerpiece of the week-long gala was an elaborate historical pageant of "Erie County – 300 Years" in the show ring, with a cast of more than 400, all residents of the county, and pupils from the Thomas Indian School who represented Indian tribes from throughout New York State.

Presiding over all was a queen picked from nominees chosen by the Board of Supervisors from across the County. She was blonde, 17-year-old Betsy Nan Muelke of Buffalo who was named "Miss Erie County." Marilyn Griffin, 18, of Williamsville was designated Miss Columbia in the pageant. The selection of "queens" became a tradition at the Fair.

Historical background for the event was written by Ralph Thorn, and narrated by Henry D. Salisbury and Walter J. MacNeil. Mr. & Mrs. Robert Colton were Directors. It was an ambitious spectacle, as described by the Buffalo Courier Express:

"A ballet representing the creation of the world opens the pageant. The story tells of the visit of the first white man to Erie County, (1626) Joseph De La Roche Daillon, a Franciscan priest; purchase of land from the Senecas; the coming of the first settler and other early immigrants; the first religious service; the first school classes; the first Erie County Fair; operation of the Underground Railway, and the marked growth of the Buffalo area during the 1890's."

"The finale engages the entire cast in summing up the events and characters prominent in the County's history." A crowd of 30,000 enjoyed the celebration.

But the 100th anniversary of the Erie County Agricultural Society was more than jubilation of the distant past.

Memories of recent wars flooded the ringside as 5,000 veterans and their auxiliary organization members paraded on the track.

"Virtually every war veterans organization in the county was represented…" reported the press. "Under huge spotlights, the marchers in bright uniforms formed a ring of color."

"Lt. Al G. Sendker of the Buffalo Police Mounted Squad led the parade… Bands and drum corps marched to such current strains as 'You Are My Sunshine', 'Over the Rainbow' and newly-introduced 'God Bless America'."

1940's

Judges E.S. Mayer of Lake View and Ross E. Brown of Holland awarded first place trophies to American Legion Drill Team from South Buffalo Post 721 and Buffalo Police Department Drum Corps and West Seneca American Legion Post 735, for the best bands. The concluding fireworks were dedicated to veterans.

Indeed war Veterans' parades would take a principle place in Society events throughout the 1940's.

The four-day horse show at the 1940 Fair set a record for size and style.

"With a sponsoring committee including many of Buffalo and Western New York's most prominent society horse fanciers, and 185 classes open to the world, the annual Erie County Agricultural Society Horse Show will be held in conjunction with the 100th anniversary!!!" said the Courier Express.

Chairman was Eugene Forrestel of Akron, with Bradley J. Hurd of Elma as co-chairman.

Trophies and prizes of more than $8,000 were awarded to the winners among 800 entries. Judges were notable: Douglas Davis, Paris, Kentucky., saddle horses; Charles Wentz, Upper Sandusky, Ohio, draft horses; Rufus C. Finch, Seabright, New Jersey, hunters and jumpers, and Mrs. John Gerken, Brooklyn, harness horse and ponies.

Heading the committees were, according to the press, "such well-known society folk and horse lovers" as: Charles K. Bassett, George E. Lattimer, Arthur G. Maddigan, Daniel H. McCarriagher, Edwin Lang Miller, Walter F. Schmidt, Roswell F. Thomas, jumpers; all of Buffalo; Mrs. Henry Mck Erb of Brooklyn; Seymour H. Knox, William C. Warren, Jr. an Mrs.

Edward G. Zeller, all of East Aurora, and Herbert C. Laub, Derby.

An interesting factor was the draft horses exhibit, the largest in the recent history of the Fair. More than 100 competed in the weight-pulling contests. Commented J.D. Burke of Cornell University, animal husbandry official: "Mechanization of the farm once threatened to eliminate the horse from the rural scene in the East, but in recent years the horse has made a comeback and now is more than holding its own in New York State.

Erie County Mounted Division formed

"The horse is back to stay because it is useful on hilly farms, can carry heavy loads for short distances more cheaply than trucks, and because its 'fuel' (food) can be produced on the farm."

One of the largest and most unusual classes that seemed to typify farm life was that of Registered Broodmares with Foal, in which Mr. Forrestel's Daisy Delphine topped the list.

(Coincidentally, the New York State Fair celebrated its centennial the following week in Syracuse.)

A record 75,507 people came to the Erie County Anniversary Fair.

And in the light of past struggle and courage, and despite generous outlays for improvements and repairs to the fairgrounds – Society had a tidy $7,419 bank balance as it faced in 1941.

Greater things were ahead. At its annual meeting of January 15, 1941, Society unanimously passed a resolution that would affect its future perhaps more drastically than any other in its history - as a drawing, sporting and financial aggrandizement.

Resting on the firm base of its "Educational, Horticultural, Mechanical and Manufacturing" interests, it would help drive the Fair down the road to the huge popularity and success it enjoys today.

As read by Director Hamilton Ward, Jr. the resolution in part follows:

"Whereas the Board of Directors of the Erie County Agricultural Society, Inc. at its regular meeting on 27th day of July 1940, did enter into an agreement with one Thomas Sheridan, whereby the Board of Directors agreed to, and did give, to Thomas Sheridan and Thomas Sheridan did take from the Board of Managers a certain option for and in consideration of the sum of seven hundred fifty dollars ($750.00), said option being for the purpose of securing a priori right to enter into an agreement with the Erie County Agricultural Society, Inc. for the use of its grounds at Hamburg, New York, for the purpose of conducting Pari-Mutuel harness racing upon certain terms and conditions…"

…under of Sheriff Art Britt in 1948

1940's

Pari-Mutuel betting, organized in 1888, is a betting pool in which those who bet on competitors finishing in the first three places share the total amount bet, minus a percentage for the management.

The conditions were "that Thomas Sheridan or his assigns, shall erect and maintain upon the grounds of the Erie County Agricultural Society, Inc. such buildings and equipment as is necessary and proper to conduct such harness races, and that such buildings and equipment shall become the property of the Erie County Agricultural Society, Inc. upon erection and installation…"

For this privilege Thomas Sheridan and/or his assigns agreed to pay Society annual rentals starting at $1,500 for the first year, and gradually increasing to $7,500 per year for five years thereafter."

The passing of the resolution is particularly memorable on two counts:

First, Society for the first time granted a second party the right to erect extensive buildings on its grounds.

Secondly, although the pari-mutuel plan was conceived long before the outbreak of WWII, the option to exercise it was formalized approximately two months after World War II

The move indicated an unprecedented expansiveness of Society to admit "a stranger within its gates," and a retention of its traditional courage in "ploughing ahead" despite threatening roadblocks.

In 1941, the Erie County Fair continued to gallop on at a record-breaking pace: 95,642 men, women and children thronged to the Fair held in the August sunshine of a peaceful Western New York. Intake was $121,216.

Throughout its history, from earliest days, Society has not been one to rest on its laurels. The vision of a bigger, better Fair has led it to continually use it monies carefully but progressively, to accomplish this end.

In the royal flush of the 1941 receipts, 3,000 feet of new fence was built along McKinley Parkway Extension, Clark Street and the rear of the grounds. A new entrance gate was erected at McKinley Parkway Extension and Quinby Boulevard. Considerable new equipment including a truck trailer, mower, sprinkler and paint sprayer were acquired, and improvement of the racehorse stables was contemplated.

But nationally, the sunshine was not to last. On December 7, 1941, Japan attacked Pearl Harbor, Hawaii; 19 ships were sunk, 2,300 died.

The next day President Roosevelt declared a war on Japan, which was to last almost four years.

Gas rationing for defense did not defeat the Erie County Fair. It wounded it, but it survived the war's first year.

With an average Fair attendance of 70,000 over a period of years, 51,000 had gathered at the 1942 Fair by Friday, the day before closing.

"Taking those figures into consideration, it is apparent things turned out much better than we had anticipated…" said a Fair Official. "The Fair itself was no record breaker, but we're not going to be behind, to the contrary we're going to come out ahead."

Exhibits rooted in the soil – which survives war and peace – were featured in the Farm Organization Day in 1942. Modern milkmaids (using milking machines) competed in a contest; there was an old-time sheep-shearing competition and a woodchopping one, to the strains of the Erie County 4-H Band.

However, the sense of war was present: "A victory aspect will be given to the program by presentation to Erie County farmers and farm children of a number of pure-bred Jersey bull calves," announced the Courier Express, "as part of the American Jersey Cattle Club plan to advance the production of what the club designates as America's greatest war and peace food – milk."

"Governor Herbert H. Lehman is honorary chairman of the committee of Victory Calf distribution…One thou-

1940's

sand bulls will be given away in the nation, with 44 as New York State's allotment and Erie County getting its proportionate share."

Popular radio announcer Roland D. Foley, known as "The Voice of the Stockyards" commented on the scene above the noise of the bullpens.

But Erie County could not entirely surrender to modern times, however alarming. In addition to a massive air raid demonstration by the entire 74th Regiment of the New York National Guard with detector units, bombing planes and searchlight batteries, "dummy" bombs, anti-aircraft guns, and of course, ambulances and nurses, Society presented a rodeo.

"Other featured attractions of the week will be the bulldogging, rope tricks and wild steer riding and many other Western Stunts," reported the press. "Thirty men and women experts and three carloads of untamed stock are used, including Brahma bulls, wildest of bovine stock."

Yet, even the Brahma bulls knew their limits: "Because the rodeo animals will not perform with elephants about, the famous Dr. Barnard Elephant Act had to be cancelled. The Marvelous Novak Sisters, aerial tumblers, substituted for them.

For the first and only time – before and since – in its 161-year history, the Erie County Agricultural Society held no fair in 1943. Harness racing at the track was discontinued from the spring of 1943 to 1945.

Meeting on April 8, 1943, in the Hotel Lafayette, Buffalo, 12 of the Society's 16 Directors first discussed the possibility of conducting a "modified" version. In the end, it was decided that if the fair could not be held in its "entirety," it would be better to drop it for a year at least.

"Omission of this year's fair will mean the first interruption in the annual farm show since the Agricultural Society was organized 103 years ago," reported the Courier Express. "Last year's fair was held in the face of a request by the Office of Defense Transportation that all fairs be cancelled. The ODT's request came so late the cancellation would have entailed a loss that Society could not have absorbed."

When horses drew the public to the fair during the Civil War, and even in World War I when everybody did not own a car – the fair went on. But the very mechanical advancement that required man-made fuel rather than animal horsepower drew the fair to a halt - the ironies of progress.

However, the gates of this pride of Erie County did not remain shut long.

"In two weeks, the Erie County Fair at Hamburg will return from vacation," announced the press on August 6, 1944. "Whether absence has made the hearts of the fans grow fonder, the management doesn't know. But it is greasing the turnstiles, just in case...

"From all indications, this is to be a banner Fair year in Erie County. Farmers, virtually imprisoned on their farms for the last two years by lack of help and the need for raising bumper wartime crops, are all set for a vacation, and have been hoarding their A coupons to go to the Fair, at least that's the picture Cyril F. Crows, County Agricultural agent, gets in his travels around the county."

Agent Crowe had it right.

"Showing few effects of the war, polio (an epidemic in progress), or even the drought (a severe one that year), the Erie County Fair which opened yesterday at Hamburg was still the old, familiar 'Hamburg Fair' of pre-war days, but all wrapped up in a new package," said the Courier Express. "This 103rd annual exposition of the County Agricultural Society holding day and night stands through Saturday, is back from a two-year vacation, no fair having been held in 1943."

Victory Gardens in the Grange Building 1944

However, there were pluses and minuses. Positively, it was a Presidential election year (Franklin D. Roosevelt running for his third term), always a big come-hither on Mayors and Politicians Day. Negatively, there was the epidemic of infantile paralysis that had swept the countryside, with 17 cases reported in neighboring Eden alone, placing it "well at the top in New York State and the nation." On the eve of the Fair, Society's board of managers regretfully called off the Children's Days program, in addition to the drought.

Yet the renewed fair bore the imprint of war. Owing to the current emphasis on food production, the Farm Organization – Farm and Home Bureaus, 4-H Clubs, Future Farmers of America, et al – joined Veterans groups – the American Legion and Veterans of Foreign Wars – in a special Buffalo Veterans and Farm Organizations Day.

There was a "munitions" exhibit and a Victory Garden display. "Food will win the war and write the peace," which replaced the usual flower show under the grandstand. Dr. Arthur J. Pratt of Cornell University who judged it awarded first prize to the Eden Garden Club.

Owing to the drought, the Fair's usual consumption of 100,000 gallons of water, supplied by the Hamburg Water Department, was cut in half.

The traditional nightly fireworks were cancelled "because Hamburg is in the same military zone as the eastern cities, when there is a ruling against serial display of fireworks."

But the flavor of the renewed Fair was largely the same. There was still a greased pig roll, a woodsawing contest, churning competitions, horseshoe pitching and bait and fly-casting. Wrestling, of course, on Saturday night.

The dove of peace survived the time of war.

1940's

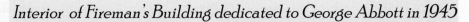
Interior of Fireman's Building dedicated to George Abbott in 1945

"The present keen interest in pigeons, a hobby which has come into its own as a result of the wartime importance of these birds as messenger carriers, was reflected in the number and variety of entries, 350 birds being listed," said the Courier Express.

A champion is a champ in war and peace. The single-combed white Leghorn, fluffy and proud, owned by Henry A. Brooker of Gardenville, lorded it from his coop as Grand Champion of poultry at the 1944 Fair.

There were new displays, harbingers of changes that would greatly affect both agriculture and horticulture.

"A graphic lesson in what soil conservation accomplishes is provided in the joint Farm Bureau and Erie County Soil Conservation District exhibit under the grandstand, " reported the press.

"In one part of the exhibit one sees a hillside where erosion really is going to town, while adjacent to it, the same hillside with corrective measures put into practice and eroding water slowed down to a walk."

It was noted further: "With several big exhibits the Farm Bureau is doing itself proud this year. Innovations will be the exhibition of record-producing cows in the County's Dairy Herd Improvement Associations, and an exhibit put on by the Artificial Breeding Associations, which have come to the fore since the last Fair."

Despite a world war in progress, the public still called for the thrill of danger. The Hollywood Hell Drivers again provided it – but with a difference:

"Lucky Teter and his famous Hell Drivers, who had become a fixture at the Fair, will not be present," the press noted. "Lucky, who carried a good luck coin and would never permit his men to perform a trick stunt until he tested it himself.ld never permit his men to perform a trick stunt until he tested it himself, was killed while stunting in Indianapolis last year."

1940's

"The Hollywood Hell Drivers, including some of Lucky's performers, will pinch-hit this year. They will do many of his stunts, without wasting rubber or gasoline. Their stunt cars will have plastic tires and burn synthetic fuel. The usual crashes and the driving of machines through fire and plate glass will be included on their bill."

Highlight of the act was Joe Chitwood, Oklahoma Indian, former Eastern AAA Champion, who circled the track on his auto at top speed, soared from a ramp and crash-drove into a parked car.

A warning from the Washington Office of Defense Transportation in the Spring of 1945, to managers of state, regional and county fairs "not to make any elaborate advance preparations for such events," owing to conservation of gasoline during the war, was countered by Jacob C. Newton, Society Secretary.

Mr. Newton explained that the Hamburg Fair is a "local" proposition serving only Erie County, and that its drawing power covers a radius of only about 20 miles; and therefore "there will be no serious drain of gasoline resources of patrons and, also, the fairgrounds are easily accessible to public transportation systems."

Anyway, by August 20th, 1945, the war was over, and when the Fair opened, gas rationing had been lifted, and the countryside breathed expansively again.

The Firemen who had been overshadowed for months by military parades were especially jubilant.

"Today will be Firemen's Day at the Erie County Fair in Hamburg," acclaimed the Courier Express, "and volunteer smoke-eaters, whose parad-

86

1940's

ing had been cramped, will celebrate with a victory parade."

The 1945 Fair marked the last showing of one of its best wartime exhibitors – the Victory gardeners, in which agriculture joined hands with patriotism to help feed a warring country.

Led by the Hamburg Band to such current favorites as "It's a Grand Night for Singing" on a Star," five State Association officers and the Erie County Board of Supervisors joined officers of the Firemen's associations of Erie, Monroe, Niagara, Allegheny, Chautauqua, Cattaraugus and Orleans counties in a triumphal march. Old-time, smoke-spewing fire engines also were on exhibition, all polished up in 1945 for the 104th Erie County Fair.

An unusual new display was the State Department of Commerce's huge exhibit shown at seven sites throughout the State, the Fair among them, to give a comprehensive picture of state government and its services. It included a graphic presentation of the State's plans for the nearly 2,000,000 Veterans returning from World War II.

A feature of this exhibit was a 10-foot electrically magnetized map, which provided the viewer with answers to 48 questions by means of push buttons.

The questions dealt with the state's historical background, topography, industrial advantages and some of the projects planned for it in the post-war era. Hidden in their midst was a plan that would change the state's history, the plan for the 450-mile Thruway between Buffalo and New York City.

1940's

At the 1945 Fair, the George Burwell Abbott Memorial Building was dedicated. Mr. Abbott was known ad "father" of Firemen's Day at the fair.

Society's annual meeting of the 1943 had eulogized George Abbott in part, thus:

"For more than twenty years, he served the eulogized Erie County Agricultural Society as Director, Vice-President or President. His sponsorship of Children's Day and Firemen's Day is a monument to his far-sighted appreciation of the public's due and the Society's welfare…Perhaps the key to his shining success may best be found in the fact that he could obtain, by frank compromise and friendly discussion, what more turbulent men failed to obtain by strife."

With the Fair's revival and renewal, a bit of crowing was in order. It's really sound not size that counts, as the Courier Express announced on August 23, 1945 – "Bantam Outcrows Weightier Rivals," said the headline.

"Sounding off once for each ounce of his weight, a gabby little bantam won the rooster crowing contest yesterday at the Hamburg Fair."

"The featherweight, a 26-ounce Silver Sebright, owned by (again the prolific) Henry A. Brooker of Gardenville, gave out 26 times in 15 minutes."

"Crowing lustily, but not so frequently, was a 25 pound heavyweight entered by Emil Abel, Athol Springs. A single – comb dark brown Leghorn, he told the world 21 timed in 15 minutes."

"Fifteen other entries of all breeds didn't crow so good." "Silver Sebright got a silver cup."

As 30,000 people – a record-breaking auto race crowd – watched in 1945, the popular Indian Joe Chitwood again drove a speedy crimson auto around the half-mile dirt track, this time to win the 1947 Erie County Fair Trophy Sweepstakes.

Chitwood roared past the checkered flag in the 20-lap, four-mile event in 8.07.35, topping the previous record of 9.25.51.

Ambitious plans by Society were afoot early in 1949: " a new grandstand, a free-act stage and finally, at least one 60-horse barn would be constructed, it was announced.

"Cost of most of the improvements will be paid by the Buffalo Raceway interests, operators of the harness race programs at the fairgrounds track," it was reported, "but ownership of the facilities will be vested in the Fair Association."

"A new grandstand section with 500 seats will be erected west of the present stand to command a view of the free-act stage and the homestretch of the track."

The overall cost was $75,000, Society and the Raceway to share the cost of the $14,900 for the new 60 x 40-foot free act stage, which would contain dressing rooms.

The stands also would include kitchen and dining facilities and space for the increased demand for concession booths. A new trailer camp would be laid out by the Raceway.

Entertainment continued to be an increasing part of the Erie County Fair. "Smash and crash" shows, such as the latest midget auto races, continued to draw big crowds. Free acts in front of the grandstand included Kitchens' Horses, comprising Prince Charming and Liberty, educated horses, two thesus monkeys, six highly trained small mules and six additional horses.

Jan Claire and Hudson did a hand on head balancing act and Reg Kehoe had his marimba players on stage, whose only rival was Bastile and his Madison Square Garden Band sounding out the current hits "Papa, Won't You Dance With Me?" and "Baby, It's Cold Outside."

But the highlight of the closing of the 40s at the 108th Erie County Fair was the dedication of the long-planned new $60,000 Women's Activities Building. Mrs. Ballard T. Clark, in a cool green and white sheer dress snipped the green silk

Inside Octagon Women's Building 1941

ribbon at the building's entrance, signifying the opening.

Reported the Courier Express: "The building took on a festive appearance with clusters of American flags draping the front and bouquets of flowers bedecking the interior, where more than a hundred exhibits (specialized categories) are reflecting activities and coming trends in the lives of Buffalo area women today."

Miss Jane H. Todd, deputy commissioner of the State Commerce Department, spoke, declaring the women's increasing interest in economics and civic affairs was changing the term "homemaker" to "homekeeper."

"The homemaker of today not only runs the mechanics of a household, brings up children and often earns money when needed, but also serves on all community councils that affect her home. Here her activity is gaining new impetus…"

Miss Todd, also head of the New York Council for Women in Business, listed motives for women entering the business, whose numbers had increased since the war, including cost of living, loss of war jobs, attitude toward age and divorce.

She appealed especially to farmwomen in financial need to start part or full-time businesses from their homes.

"The farm is emerging as a great new discovered land for the skills of women…" Miss Todd said. "Today, farm and rural women are branching out into highly commercial and profitable fields with the farm as their offices."

She told of one women whose specialty was frozen turkeys and birds, stuffed, foil-wrapped and ready for the

1940's

oven; another raised and bottled herbs; a third grew flowers and arranged them in corsages for Cornell University co-eds.

Department of Commerce workers were present to counsel women in starting their own business.

This day, August 18th, 1949, was a long hitch from that day in May 1866, when Society's minutes recorded that a Ladies Department would be formed "to be under the supervision of officers chosen by the Ladies of the Society." Time's second hand had swept from the welcomed appearance of the Triumph Washing Machine of the 1870s to women's suffrage in the 1920s to Rosie the Riveter and the businesswoman of the 1940s.

"To the bright hopes of the future!" declared Miss Todd – a future that would surpass her imagination.

END of 1940's

just few lines to [...] 8

the coming fair season 19[...]

[...] now closing contracts wit[...]

[...] see, last season we played [...]

[...]ingville. N.Y. for the firemen[...]

[...]vention, and called you up [...]

[...] if we could book with yo[...]

[...] we were too late, so now [...]

[...]ing to you before I'll be too la[...]

[...]st bought a new 1924 thr[...]

[...]ast merry-go-round from Alla[...]

[...]schell, and new 1924. Ferris wh[...]

[...] Eli Bridge Co. also I have [...]

[...]d Athletic Show and will h[...]

[...]more show before then[...]

Part Three
Harvesting

"Divine Nature gave the fields, human art built the cities"
Marcus Terentius Varra, 116-27 B.C.

Remembering the Past
Embracing the Future
Chapter 12

Like the mounting power of industrialization throughout the nation, the Erie County Agricultural Society went into an all-time high in the mid-20th century.

Availability of scientifically advanced farm equipment and the great mercantile resources of neighboring Buffalo – now with a population of 522,759 – as well as the opportunity the annual fair offered merchants to display goods to thousands, moved the Fair itself, into place in 1951, as one of the largest enterprises in Erie County, and second among county fairs in New York State, surpassed only by the Queens-Nassau Fair in Mineola.

Not only did the Fair rise to the new industrial and commercial display heights, but the performance of the Buffalo Philharmonic Orchestra on its stage on August 15 lifted it once and for all – above the roofs of stables, carnival tents and

A busy day for the Midway

1950's

93

Poultry Judging 1951

organizational marching bands. At this single event field and city – both intrinsically and interdependently – recognized the fact, and joined in spiritual as well as literal harmony. The very descriptions of the Fair in the newspapers throughout the '50's testified to the expanded interests and homogenization of the enterprise. Here are a few:

"The 110th Annual Erie County Fair (1951) will feature an expanded exhibit program designed to reflect the industrial, farming and home interests of Erie County and the Niagara Frontier, it was announced yesterday by Clayton C. Taylor of Lawtons."

"The 110th exposition plans a six-day and six-night program throwing the spotlight on Erie County agricultural, home and industrial interests."

Again, at the 112th Exhibit, "here under canvas and in exhibit halls thousands of displays from farm, home, business and industry of the Niagara Frontier, will thrill fairgoers."

By 1959, the 118th Erie County Fair was termed " a common denominator for city, urban and rural farm life.

But the Erie County Agricultural Society did not forget the past. In the 1950s, the History Department of the Fair

The *"Wild Mouse"* coaster debuted in the 1950's

was established through the interests of Society treasurer George G. Sipprell and Mrs. Julia Boyer Reinstein, president of the recently founded Erie County Historical Federation.

Nurtured by Mrs. Reinstein, co-superintendent with Mr. Sipprell, it grew from a simple display of maps and pictures in a corner of the Firemen's Building in 1952 through various sites to its own building in 1958.

Formally dedicated by Lynda Bird Johnson, daughter of President Lyndon B. Johnson, at the Fair's International Goodwill Day, August 23, 1965, the new building had 19 exhibition areas for competitive displays by county historical societies. By the early '70s, more than 60,000 people were visiting its well-researched exhibitions annually.

Display cases, counsel and an occasional exhibit were provided to the burgeoning department by the Buffalo Historical Society, now the Buffalo and Erie County Historical Society that shares superintendence with the Erie County Historical Federation.

Pasture and city gates opened to each other. The "lowing herd" joined the world of machines and cash registers. Perhaps the dominant reason for the success of the Fair as it entered the 1950's was expressed by Eugene P. Forrestel of Akron when taking office as President in 1953:

"The Erie County Fair is big business," he said, "because it is an Erie County tradition, enthusiastically accepted by all interests – farmers, business people, schools, city and rural residents."

It was big business but it was, as it always had been, a circulating business.

"Although Big Business – the Erie County Fair has a capital investment of $1,500,000

Lynda Bird Johnson
August 23, 1965

1950's

Motorized Sideshow –
The "Motordrome"

in buildings and grounds and does an annual business of nearly a quarter of a million dollars – it is a case of going in one pocket and out the other, "wrote farm reporter LeRoy E. Fess in the Courier Express. "This fund and more too, is paid out annually in premiums."

A vital announcement was made also in 1953 concerning the Fair in the press:

The Erie County Fair is out of debt. "Mortgages, cancelled bills and other red ink items were burned yesterday (January 21, 1953), at the County Agricultural Society's 112th annual meeting in Grange Hall, Hamburg.

"Announcing the Fair organization's debt-free status, Treasurer George G. Sipprell said not only was he able to liquidate all outstanding obligations out of the 1952 income ($230,502), but the Society at the close of the fiscal year Dec. 1, had a bank balance of $22, 423.07."

The 1953 Fair broke all-time records almost across the board.It was typical of Society's modus operandum through the years that it now pressed on. The spirit and courage that had advanced it through more than a century of mortgages and loans, now with vision and vigor, continued to propel it forward into its second century.

JAMES E.
STRATES SHOWS, INC.

PICTURE REVIEW OF THE MOST PHOTOGRAPHED MIDWAY ON EARTH

Home Office
N. Y.

Fiscal Offices
42 INSURANCE BUILDING
UTICA, N. Y.

Winter Quarters
ORLANDO, FLA.

1950's

The Buffalo Evening News Suburban League
Championship Baseball Game

George Lohr
Exhibitor for 50 years at the Fair

A capital improvement program of $48,000 – the largest in the Fair's history – was immediately launched, and new sheep and swine barns, bleachers, dressing rooms under the grandstand stage, sewage improvements, fences and parking lot spaces were built or developed.

Even then, at the end of a three-year period, a $40,000 surplus graced the books, which George Sipprell said would enable Society "to take a possible rainy fair (with its inevitable loss of gate) in stride."

"During the last five years (1951-58) the Fair Society has spent an excess of $143,000 in improvements, repairs and additions..." reported the Courier Express at the opening of 1956.

And for the first time, the Fair was extended to an 8-day run, with great success. A record of more than 300,000 persons attended, and an unprecedented $40,000 in premiums and prizes were dispensed.

But as the crowds increased so did the needs and goals of Society. Always ahead were demands of upkeep and dreams of expansion.

By January 1957, the Buffalo Evening News reported: "The need for a $200,000 capital improvement program at the Erie County Fairgrounds was outlined today in the treasurer's report of the Erie County Agricultural Society...the program would include a permanent Industrial Building."

Big business, indeed. As the 111th Fair opened in 1952, Society listed 600 members and an additional 400 in the Women's Department, who did not vote, but had autonomous operation of their section.

Despite its size, the Association had only one full-time salaried member, William Bieler, Superintendent of Grounds, who lived on the premises the year-round in a Society-owned house. Fifty buildings on the 160-acre tract were under his care.

The seven officers and nine Directors who managed the Fair, continued, as in the past, to serve without pay, the Secretary, Treasurer and Public Relations Director alone, receiving only expenses.

It was this volunteer spirit throughout its history, this club-like ambiance, this assemblage of squires – many of whose grandsires have sat in those same chairs – that has given the Erie County Agricultural Society its rare vintage and pre-eminence.

1950's

In 1956 the United States adopted the motto "In God We Trust," and the first transatlantic telephone cable crossed the Atlantic.

The freedom and energy of solvent Society was reflected in its exhibits, as were the trends of a rapidly changing world. The Fair began to reach out nationally – beyond its county and even state boundaries.

The E.I. Pont de Nemours Co. found the fair a suitable setting for a safety show calling the attention of thousands of the public to "the nearly 100,000 deaths in 1950 on farm, in home and through traffic and industrial accidents."

There was a $1 million farm equipment exhibit sponsored by the Erie County Farm Equipment Dealers Association, as instructive but also a strong sales pitch for manufacturers across the country.

As the county became increasingly "health conscious," the former Women's Department Octagon building was encircled in 1957 with nearly 20 health displays by national, state and area health agencies, showing services that were increasing the life-span of farmer and city dweller alike by more than 20 years since the turn of the century. They ranged from cancer, heart ailments and arthritis to medical, dental and pharmaceutical therapeutics. Facts about alcoholism as a newly recognized disease were presented.

It was a long way from the days of patent medicine and "home" remedies.

Civic bodies such as the Erie County Planning Board and the Buffalo and Erie County Public Library also exhibited. Local food producers too shone.

"There were so many people here today who had trouble getting in to set up our own exhibits," said Otto E. Jensen, chairman of the board of the Grocery Manufacturers Representatives of Buffalo, in charge of a giant "Food Fair" in 1953.

Housed under a 190-foot-long tent were 36 booths showing products "from the newly-introduced pizza to pot cleaners"; 60,000 samples were given out.

Pinpointing produce grown nearby, the Bailey-Clinton Market displayed its wares in the Agricultural Building.

Burlesque Shows were a popular attraction in the 1950's on the Midway

Open Dairy Cattle Show

1950's

Gov. Harriman congratulates the 1957 Grand Champion Beef Steer Exhibitor

It was significant too, that the State Government doffed its hat to Society in 1957, but the visit of Gov. Averill Harriman to the Fair – the first governor to visit the exhibition since the turn of the century.

But the most notable display of the 1950s was the first Industry Show Tent, with booths indicating industry's contributions to the employment level and economy of Erie County by exhibition of industrially produced products. The dreamed-of industrial building was yet to come.

The show was Society's recognition of man-made rather than naturally produced wares, and in turn, industry's need of the farm as well as city population.

It would take both farm and city to produce the mammoth exhibition that would eventually establish the Erie County Fair and Exhibition as the largest county fair in the nation.

1950's

Balancing all this technique and salesmanship was the continued popularity and increase of entertainment at the Fair. Raising crops and stocks is labor – no matter how devoted one is to land and barn – but hitting a target for a teddy bear or watching a "thrill show" of autos which defied all highway laws was release, fun, a chance to laugh and wonder. Nor were "city folk" exempt.

The James E. Strates Shows Midway was now over a mile long.

"The words big and new must be written over Hamburg Fair this year," reported the Courier Express in 1951. "You get the impression the minute you enter the grounds. Maybe it's the multiple ferris wheels on the Midway. Instead of the usual one, there are four in a row all turning at once."

Wardinski hot dog stand on Midway 1953

Antique Car Race at the Fair

Again in 1955: "It was a perfect day for a fair at the Erie County Expositions' 114th annual opening…warm enough to make the lemonade flow; cool enough to give an appetizing aroma to frying onions and hot dogs…The mile-long midway with its myriad bazaars, hawkers, food and notion stands was a page out of Arabian Nights."

There was more sophisticated entertainment:

A convertible stock car blasted from the mouth of a cannon.

Old-timers who remembered the "Tin Lizzie," the first Ford, enjoyed the Fair's first display of road hardy antique auto-mobiles. How time passes! Arranged by the Lake Erie Region Antique Automobile Club and the Horseless Carriage Club, the 14 all road worthy cars formed a parade around the racetrack in the evenings. Among them were an Imperial, 1894; a Warren-Detroit and a Maxwell, 1911; Ford touring car, 1913; Moon touring car, 1921; Auburn Phaeton, 1932. By 1958, as the first U.S. satellite, Explorer I, went into orbit, the parade had enlisted 100 antique cars.

Fireworks had lit up the Fair since its early days, but the five United States wars it had survived had left their mark. It was now the custom to touch off an aerial bomb salute to open the Fair.

There were gentler things. Another new opening feature in 1951 was the release of 2000 homing pigeons from a 50 —mile radius in mass flight in front of the grandstand by the Niagara Frontier Pigeons Fanciers Association and the Buffalo Racing Pigeons Combine.

Delicious food and a succession of famous and interesting guests gracefully appeared, which helped to launch the hus-band and wife team of Bill and Mildred Miller, owners of a large turkey farm in Colden, into the limelight and great popu-larity throughout Western New York, Southern Ontario and Northern Pennsylvania.

1950's

One of the most popular presentations at the Fair was the broadcast from its grounds of the "Meet the Millers," a food and talks show program that appeared five days a week on WBEN-TV, from 1950 to its retirement in 1971.

Ultimately, "Meet the Millers," the first locally produced TV show to appear in color "outrated" such national offerings as Merv Griffin, Art Linkletter and soap operas.

An attraction of the '50s too was the annual amateur show, sponsored by area farm organizations, in which boys and girls up to age 21 tried out for performance in the grandstand at the Fair. Prizes were awarded to the winners chosen by the audience. Donald Hackle of Station WGR headed the show. Democratic America seems to need a king and queen at gala events. Society was no exception. A queen of the Fair was chosen in 1958 to be the "beauty and personality" representative of Western New York. But a juvenile royal pair between 14 and 17 years of age was selected to reign on Children's Day. Their specifications were broader based: "You can have freckles and straight hair and still be king or queen at the Erie County Fair," noted the Buffalo Evening News.

"Beauty and muscles will not be the basis for choosing the 'Recreation King and Queen' of Children's Day…Judging

1950's

MIKE OLSEN
Lot Superintendent

WAYNE KINGSLEY
Supt. of Diesels

MATINEE TIME

It takes romance—adventure—thrills—color—noise—music—to draw crowds. Always so
of patrons wherever its tents go up and its bright lights flash out "Welcome." Whether it

1950's

JAMES YOTAS
Supt. of Construction

O. L. Stonecipher
Chief Electrician

thing new and different. The James E. Strates Shows is proud of its record in attracting thousands and thousands day or not—crowds jam the world's most favorable known midway.

1950's

will be on participation in hometown community recreation activities, popularity, sportsmanship, personal accomplishments and (lastly) personal appearances."

A sign of advancing times was that among the class displays of Buffalo and Erie County Schools in the Education Building, industrial arts took its place among history in the fine arts.

With an eye to posterity – the lifeline of farming – Society gave particular emphasis to youth in the '50s.

A $47,000 Junior Building was established in 1959.

"In the Junior Exhibit Departments farm youth will compete for more than $7,000 in cash awards for farm produce, livestock, and homecraft products," reported the Courier-Express.

The value of the granges in presenting the farm picture also drew special attention.

Breaking away from the traditional display of fruit, vegetables, grains and canned fruit, Holland Grange presented "Evolution in the Kitchen," an exhibit illustrated by old and modern cooking utensils placed side by side.

Boston Grange, with the theme"They Grew it First and Ate it First," showed the homeland of all today's common foods – fruits, vegetables and condiments – by means of an arrangement of ribboned placards. Cherries were from Japan, grapes from Persia, and olives from Greece. American Indians, it was noted, first grew raspberries. Lawtons Grange compared haying methods of today and yesterday. Springville Grange presented a display of wedding gowns over the past 200 years, while Marilla Grange enumerated crops grown at different periods of the country's history.

Free admission to all children up to age 16 and an advanced sale of seasonal ticket books at $2.75 for adults was granted in 1952.

The hundreds of children now attending the Fair called for supervision and care. A Buffalo hospital rose to the occasion:

"Children's Hospital again will provide a first aid and lost child tent at the 110th Erie County Fair, "announced the press in 1951. "Each day a doctor, registered nurse and two occupational therapists will be on duty from 10 a.m. to 10 p.m."

"Moir P. Tanner, hospital Director, ... urged that all children under 14 wear an identification tag fastened to their clothing."

Dr. Bernard Eisenberg, director of the Children's Lost and Found, reported more than 20 children had been brought there on Children's Day in 1953. The children were given books, lollipops and games to amuse them until their parents were located by loudspeaker from the grandstand.

Children look with amazement at the Baby Chick Hatchery

1950's

Competition on the racetrack, in the stable or the barn is always a major ingredient of a Fair. It both inspires participants' desire to excel and teaches them how to achieve it.

The Erie County Fair and Exhibition bustled with winners and "champs" as the '50s advanced: The more than $7,000 purses in harness racing by 1951; the Courier Express Championship Trophy for the Erie County Young Harmonizers Quartet Championships, sponsored by the area Barbershop Quartet Chapters; the Buffalo Evening News Golden Horseshoe (pitching) Contest for boys; sanctioned sprints by the Buffalo Bicycle Racing Club and big car racing with national drivers at the wheel. And the continual heated contest of Veterans and Firemen's parades.

Lest nature be outdone, mule races were introduced at the 1957 Fair, but the Conservation of the land and care of its wildlife also received increased exhibition space and attention.

But the warp and woof of farm-based activities, the enhancement of stock and crops, the respect for the hand-made, the emphasis on the farm as a citadel stood firm for the Erie

County Agricultural Society even as radio resounded over the fields and television invaded the farmhouse.

Many reasons are given for the success of the Erie County Fair down its 150 years – vision. Yankee thrift, German diligence, hard work, devoted volunteers, and an effort to meet current public taste. But surely this land-based quality, this "founding of human civilization," as Daniel Webster put it, this desire to draw sustenance from the land by crops, livestock and homespun arts has struck a powerful response in countryside and city.

Flushed with its liberation from debt and the breaking of all-time records, Society opened its gates for a "sneak preview" on Sunday, August 14, 1955, its first time receiving the public on the Sabbath. An estimated 11,500 attended. A year later, the first 8-day fair, which would start a precedent, took place to a record crowd of more than 300,000. New picnic areas in tree-shaded groves for family groups – many of whom brought their own lunch baskets – were opened in 1958.

Provident even in mellow August, the Amherst Garden Club told viewers how to "Put Your Garden to Sleep," demonstrating ways to make plants snug for the winter, and offering such hints as covering pansies with cottony-looking glass mulch and building slanting covers to keep snow from flattening rhododendrons.

Indifferent to the cold, the first in the area were the Scotch-Highland cattle shown by Stewart Williamson of Hamburg.

1950's

"It is the first time this breed has ever been shown locally," reported the press. "Williamson is the only owner in the State of these squat, shaggy, long-haired red cattle."

"Because of their hardiness and ability to withstand cold winter temperatures, the Scotch-Highland or a cross of them will be the leading beef cattle herd in America within 20 years," predicted Williamson.

A Buf Orpington hen was the "Grand Champ" of the poultry show. She came from the coops of W.L. Mullaney of Orchard Park, who had 16 winners in the show. "Some of the Flemish rabbits resemble small kangaroos," commented the press of the hutches. Loyalty to the Fair had been ingrained in Hamburg townsfolk for generations. The following was typical:

"Peering out from under a battered felt hat, George H. Frazier figured he had painted 35 signs yesterday, to direct fair visitors everywhere from the sheep barns to the auto show," said the Courier Express at the 1953 Fair.

"A barber in Hamburg, Frazier has hung a closed sign on his shop in order to swing his paintbrush for the Fair, a job he has done for 28 years…"

Society closed its 1950's Fair with exhibits in 35 departments, premiums of more than $40,000 – from $1 for an antique snuffbox to $125 for a winning horse-pull – and by the presentation of a $25,000 horse, courtesy, Niagara Frontier Builders Association.

To top it all off Gene Autry, his horse champion and his Western troupe, rope-trick, bull whip and bareback riders, per-

Scottish Highland cattle 1958

1950's

formed before the grandstand.

Not to be outdone by the recent launching of the USS Nautilus, the first atomic-powered submarine, the Erie County Sheriff's Department staged an aquatic show, including skin diving, in the pool near the Conservation Building as Explorer I, first U.S. Satellite, soared over the farms and cities of Erie County, New York, the Erie County Agricultural Society – with increasingly sophisticated techniques of husbandry, nationally acclaimed entertainment and progressive civic display – wound on, merging the interests of town and farm that would lead it to the green pastures of eminence it occupies among United States county fairs today.

End of 1950's

1950's

of the coming

I am now clos

fair sec, last se

Springville. N.Y.

convention, and

here if we could

but we were too

writing to you bef

just bought

breast merry-go-

Attracting the World
Chapter 13

The Erie County Agricultural Society welcomed the world in the 1960s. In cooperation with the Buffalo International Institute, an organization devoted to the welcoming and assistance of foreign-born people began in 1964 at the 127th Fair, as follows:

"Among the new attractions at the nation's second largest County Fair," reported the Courier-Express, "is an International Trade Fair sponsored by the U.S. Customs Service and featuring household goods from 15 nations, products imported and exported locally, and custom inspection and law enforcement techniques."

The Customs Service, manning the passage across the Niagara River between neighboring Buffalo and the Canadian shore, is a powerful presence in Erie County. "Other attractions of the trade fair," continued the report, "are twice-nightly performances by local nationality groups of native dancers and music arranged by the International Institute of Buffalo."

1960's

111

A Stroll Down the Avenue of Flags

It was noted that many of the displays of native costumes and household items were provided to the trade fair by the consulates of the nations they represent.

Custom exhibits showed the work of the service in inspecting and testing imported goods, and how the service enforces the laws regulating Federal Agencies such as the Food & Drug Administration, the Internal Revenue Service and the Department of Agriculture.

In a county of nearly one million people descended largely from immigrants, the interest in such a show was a natural. Instruction in the function of federal agencies also proved valuable to a population far removed from their national seat in Washington.

By the 1966 Fair, displays from 40 foreign countries animated the grandstand exhibition hall. Typical of the lands represented were Albania, Austria, Brazil, Bolivia, Finland, France, England, Germany, Israel, Japan, Poland, the Philippines and Thailand. Ten international airlines also joined the show. To cap the exhibit, a day was designated International Goodwill Day. Dignitaries from several foreign countries attended.

Not to forget the United States, an Avenue of Flags was presented, lined with the official flags of our then, 50 states. It should be mentioned that the international influence of the Erie County Fair reached people far from the trade show.

The Rev. Joseph P. Waclawski, now a monsignor and pastor of St. Barnabas Church in Depew, was pastor of the Roman Catholic Diocese of Buffalo's first mission parish, St. Pius X, on a hillside overlooking La Paz, Bolivia, about 7,000 miles from Erie County. He fashioned his own version of the Fair there in 1967, attracting more than 25,000 visitors to an exhibit that featured 55 adobe booths.

"It was really a fair of practical ideas," Father Waclawski told the press. "We tried to show them how to make things for themselves – to prepare food, to make and use adobe stoves, to make triple-decker bunks, to use water filters, to sanitate

1960's

through garbage and sewer disposals, and to make and use water pumps."

"We had displays on nutrition, and made a big hit with the chickens. We had chickens all the same age on display, and showed how different feed made them different in size, and superior in plumpness and succulence." The Peace Corps, the local junta (legislature), the area Agricultural Department, minister of Health and US AID assisted.

But, as ever, Society cherished its own land, the actuality of which was 160 acres, and seat of 55 buildings in 1964.

Tradition and nostalgia rises in Society's ranks at intervals down the years. An example was the revival in 1964 of a tour by its directors of the grounds on the fair's opening day – each carrying a cane. Louis E. Willet, president from 1921 to 1935, established the custom.

"The tour was conducted by all 16 directors," explained George G. Sipprell, Fair treasurer, of the revival, "and Mr. Willet ordered each of them to wear a hat and identifying badge and also carry a cane. He considered the cane to be a symbol of dignity and responsibility."

Although the official purpose of the cane was to make the directors easily recognizable to fair visitors, underlying this purpose was a desire of the president, "Mr. Willet likes to have a cane with him so he could point out the exhibits that

Douglas Leroy & Herbert Haller of Cheektowaga are delighted by the wax museum on the James E. Strates midway in 1962

1960's

113

were acceptable to him," added Mr. Sipprell. "Those he disliked were taken down immediately."

Current Fair President Harry H. Sylvester commented: "of course, when Mr. Willet took his official tour, there were only one dozen structures, and the tour could be completed in two hours."

"Today…it would be a gigantic task for all of us to inspect the whole fair in two hours. It would take that long to get through one building."

It is noteworthy that there were a record 1,980 exhibitors at the 1964 Erie County Fair, who displayed 15,041 entries.

The variety of new buildings on the fairgrounds in the 1960's illustrated the extensive widening interest of Society and its response to public taste. They ranged from grassroot farming display areas to a Historical Building to an Indian Village, all opened with appropriate ceremonies.

An $175,000 Agricultural and Grange Building was opened on August 28 1964. It was an acclamation by Society of its continued belief in the yield of field and barn in a fast motorizing world; a manifestation of Society's heart – husbandry – in the midst of all extracurricular activities on the grounds; a pledge of allegiance to the function for which Society was named. It culminated years of discussion and planning by Society and Grange and members. Arthur H. Davis was the architect.

Focal point of the "cathedral-like" building, as it was termed by the press, was the entrance of paneled glass, 40 feet wide and 35 feet deep, with indirect lighting and a display of plantings. A marble fountain donated by Michael B. Brooks, a vice president of the Fair, stood at the center.

The main exhibition hall, 169 by 63 feet, was lined with booths for Grange Exhibits and centered by display islands for fruits, vegetables and commercial produce. Folding doors could convert the main hall into three meeting rooms and a 35-foot wing housed a kitchen.

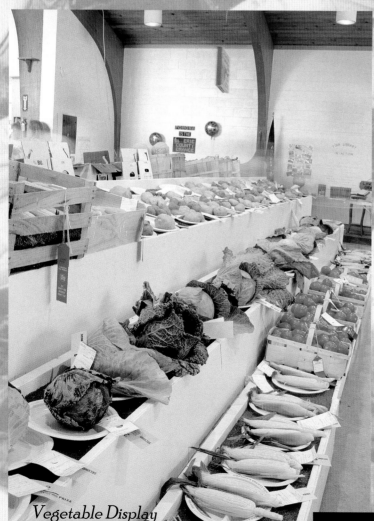

Vegetable Display

Illustrative of its prosperity was the fact that Society paid for the building in cash. An interesting note that presaged developments 25 years later was this announcement by the Buffalo Courier Express:

"Part of the building will be heated for year-round use to provide the first such facility on the fairgrounds."

It was Society's first outreach to an extended season of operations.

One of the most charming buildings on the fairgrounds is the Mount Vernon Building, a replica of George Washington's house on the Potomac.

Originally erected in 1888, and under the auspices of the Women's Department known as Floral Hall, the white, green-shuttered edifice, with its stately pillars and overhanging balcony, was dedicated at the 125th Fair in 1964 as Erie County Parks and Recreation Hall.

The new Indian Village was far older in inspiration than Mount Vernon. The inclusion of the village as an integral part of the Fair on August 22, 1965 was particularly significant in the light of the early seat of the Seneca Nation in Western New York, and the neighboring reservation at Brant, Erie County.

Reported the Buffalo Evening News:

"Members of the Seneca Nation danced, sang and formally dedicated the Fair's new Indian Village, Nyah-Weh."

"Let this village encourage new interest in the colorful and rich lore of the Indians," said the Rev. David Owl, as he formally dedicated the village whose name means 'Thank You.'

"The symbols of the American Indian are buckskin and eagle feathers," he noted, "but they are also generosity and hospitality, honesty and physical courage, a love of liberty and a desire for peace."

Mr. Seneca, president of the Council of Seneca Nations, expressed hope that the new village would bring "better

Mount Vernon Building
1964

understanding of the Senecas and their culture."

Members of the All-Seneca American Legion Post 1587 were the color guard at the ceremonies.

The whole aspect of the Fair became more sophisticated in the 1960s. There was the lovely "Dancing Waters" display in 1961, a lavish electronically controlled water show, 60 feet long and 20 feet wide.

"Operated by a man who sits at a console control panel, streams of water swirl into such dance motions as waltz and tango," described the Buffalo Courier Express. "The swaying waters have multi-colored illumination and are accompanied by music…It was first shown in this country at Radio City Music Hall…"

There were the Two Linares in stunts on wire; the Four Bizzaros who played Italian melodies by bells attached to their

1960's

Mummer's Parade

hats, arms and legs, Joyce and her Parisian Poodles, and the acrobatic Sensational Leighs.

Hubert Castle's International Circus offered 30 animals in action, and Don Ameche's International Showtime Circus performed; 1,000 balloons carrying $4 worth of admission tickets were released.

A grander than ever parade, a huge "Funfaironade" march of bands, floats, military units, costumed marchers, and sky divers opened the 1967 Fair, preceded by flag raising ceremonies and the traditional bomb salute.

The demand for military demonstrations and the desire of service unit to march continued. A Firemen's Parade in 1964 had 128 units and 3,276 marchers and prizes were awarded for the firemen, drum corps and women's auxiliaries.

The prize-winning John Fralinger String Band from the Philadelphia Thanksgiving Mummer's Parade also joined the Fair march in 1967.

Reported the Buffalo Evening News: "The parade will start at Main and Lake Streets in Hamburg shortly after 11 a.m. and will pass the grandstand about an hour later."

"Twenty-six musical groups including the United Stated Navy Band are already signed up…There will be 60 floats and eight marching units, including a newly-organized Indian group."

Not to be outdone, the Girl Scouts commemorated their 50th anniversary that year, with a pageant, "The Promise of Girl Scouting," and songs by a 150-voice choir..

The geography of the now sprawling Fair and its logistics were defined and improved.

A map of the grounds released in August 1967, showed 71 locations. A colorful trackless train with canopied

coaches now connected key sites, joining an authentic motorized San Francisco Cable Car which carried passengers about the grounds at Fair time, and also toured the seven counties of Western New York at public events and benefits.

Gaslights to create a Gay 1890's atmosphere in the newly opened Slade Park, a memorial to the late Frank S. Slade, former Society secretary and County Treasurer, and a concourse through it were proposed in 1964.

The great growth of the Fair is reflected by the innovations listed for the year 1967 alone, as reported by the press:

* *Naming of Monday of Fair Week as Senior Citizens Day, as well as the former International Good Will Day. Reduced rates to senior group clubs.*

* *Completion of the new Conservation Building, which was begun in 1966; the Buffalo Museum of Science and the State Conservation Department to provide exhibits with a live beaver in the adjoining pond.*

* *Premiums to be awarded for Indian handiwork in beads and silver, canoes and bows at the Indian Village, now sponsored by all four Western New York reservations.*

* *The Iroquois Brewing Co. will be host at a free dance, including a polka and square dance contest.*

* *A clown will parachute from a plane before the grandstand on opening after*

* *Two-hour-long band concerts in Slade Park, directed by Clayton Fattey, will be increased to two a day.*

* *Draft horses, absent from the fairgrounds for 20 years, will perform again in old-fashioned six horse hitches.*

* *Expansion of the international exhibits to 61 displays. A special exhibit of watches to be imported from Switzerland. Other presentations include a karate demonstration, Tijuana Band and a Japanese floral arrangement class.*

* *WBEN will broadcast live radio programs from the grounds, supplemented by the popular, longstanding TV program "Meet the Millers."*

* *All employees on the midway will wear uniforms.*

* *Illuminating the past, the Historical Building exhibited such various titles as "Our First Newspaper — the Aurora Standard": Clarence "Toys of the Past" (of wood, metal, glass, and china); "Early School Days in Eden (back to 1812)"; Hamburg, "Very Ancient History" (fossil collections found near 18 Mile Creek), and "The Village Smithy" (history of the Roloff blacksmith shop with tools).*

1960's

Sounds of Farming—WBEN farm reporter Al Fox carries his portable tape recorder into the barn of a Western New York dairy farm to record a story for his early morning radio listeners in 1961.

Two other historic features were celebrated: In 1967, a marker commemorating the long history of the Fair, held in Buffalo from 1820 to 1850, and then in various Western New York area towns until coming to the present Hamburg site. The marker was erected at the original location of the Fair there in 1868. It was noted at ceremonies that the Erie County Fair was the oldest civic community organization in Erie County.

The 100th anniversary of the Fair's establishment in Hamburg was celebrated by a pageant on the grounds on Opening Day in 1965, in cooperation with the Town and Village of Hamburg.

With premiums running in excess of $50,000 since 1963, the Fair was extended to a 9-day event

1965
Grand Champion Holstein
Chris Schintzius
10 years old

1965
Grand Champion Baby Beef
Bob Fuller

1960's

in 1969, from August 15 to 23. Perhaps in gratitude for blessings bestowed, an Interfaith Service was held at the last 60's fair.

"All activity ceased along the midway, animal barns and horse show ring at the Erie County Fair Sunday (August 17, 1969)," reported the Buffalo Courier Express, "as an interfaith religious service took place before the grandstand. Shiloh First Baptist Church choir sang and Catholic, Protestant and Jewish clergymen took part in the service, with Vincent Y. Bowditch, regional director of the National Association of Christians and Jews, delivering the address."

The Erie County Sheriff's Mounted Patrol 1962

The Erie County Sheriff's Mounted Unit stood at attention by the temporary pulpit.

There are always "special people" at the Erie County Fair. Like Leroy H. Lockwood, 32, of Eden who was picked as "the outstanding young farmer of the year," 1963, by the Hamburg Junior Chamber of Commerce. With modern soil practices he increased his yield more than 33 percent, upped his dairy herd from 12 to 34 head, and his chickens from 250 to 3,200.

Youngest farming couple present in the grandstand were Mr. & Mrs. Earl Gingerich of East Aurora, both about 21. On

1960's

the other end of the life scale were the George Phitzingers of Eden in their mid-80's, who had been farming all their lives.

The Pomona Grange John W. Kleis Award for a youth in farming went to 21-year-old Andrew Johnston of Springville, a victim of cerebral palsy, who raised heifers.

Of course there are also special moments at every fair. One has been the arrival of the James E. Strates Shows, Inc. Its arrival in 1965 as reported by the press:

"The 50 car carnival train (described as the biggest in the country) arrived in Hamburg at 8 p.m. Sunday night…The bright-painted cars and wild animals lent an old-time circus train atmosphere to the unloading proceedings, which lasted until 6 a.m. Monday morning. Hamburg youngsters crowded around…"

1960's

"I had these wipper snappers all the time"
whispers Rutheford H. Farrar, 83 of Eden

Pictured with Mrs. Manuel Gomez &
Mrs Herbert Draudt
1962.

On a more classical level, in 1969 the Fair began offering performances by community theater groups in an outdoor theater on the Avenue of the Flags.

Participating groups were the Williamsville Circle Theater, Clarence Players, Towne Players, East Aurora Players, Hamburg Little Theater, Ira Aldridge Players and The Island Theater.

Shows from "Musical Comedy Man – An Evening with George M. Cohan" to an old-fashioned melodrama, "He Ain't Done Right by our Nell" to "Spoon River Anthology" were presented.

Little Grace notes from field and barn at the Fair in the 60s included such pleasantries as a new type of squash called "turban squash," resembling a Turkish headdress, grown by Walter Henry of Eden; a week-old bull calf owned by Edward Kazmarek of Alden; the tiny rabbit of 7-year-old Kim Hodson of Orchard Park, which she had fed first with an eyedropper, then by the doll's bottle – until it grew to size and won a blue ribbon, and Marion B. Tayler's nine Berkshire pigs only 7 days old and 11 of his Chester Whites, a large white hog, 15 days. They made the trip to the Fair from South Byron, NY penned in chicken wire.

To the animal lover and sentimentalist, the animal baby beef auction is traumatic. But the raising of livestock for human consumption is a realistic part of farm life.

In 1963, for example, 60 cattle were sold at the Fair for $16,249.97. Such sales can be productive: William Henry, 12 of Eden, whose grand champion black Angus sold for $1,032.55, "the highest price paid in many years," planned "to put his money in the bank and perhaps raise more cattle," noted the press. Life goes on.

As the 60s drew to a close, Anne McIlhenny Matthews, columnist for the Buffalo Courier-Express, described the Women's Department at the Fair:

"Watching this group of remarkable women and their youthful assistants set up shop…was an education in low-voiced, pleasant efficiency…"

It takes two days to enter the exhibits and one day to carry them home. Considering that the entries number upward of 4,000, it is amazing that there have been no thefts and a minimum of lost or strayed entries over the many years…"

1960's

Nor was the department strictly for women; 18 percent of the entries in the hooked rugs, carvings and afghans sections were entered by men.

So as U.S. Astronaut Neil A. Armstrong, commander of the Apollo 11 mission, became the first man to set foot on the moon on June 20, 1969 – the Erie County Fair, in its own earthbound but steady way, drew a record crowd of 78,975 men, women and children at its 136th annual Fair. They traversed it by a new open glider car.

The public scene however, was changing: At the opening of the Agri-Grange Building in 1964, Clayton C. Taylor of Lawtons, one of two Directors of the Fair who still made his living farming, said, "The number of farmers is always dropping, although the Grange is trying to keep up interest…"

William Bensley, New York Farm Bureau president, said the role of a county fair was to act as "a go-between" for farmers and persons living in urbanized areas.

As the strains of the Marine Corps Band from Washington filled the fairgrounds in 1968, Benjamin DeYoung Jr., Erie County Fair President, predicted the fair would match its first century of growth at Hamburg with another century of growth.

As the decade closed he said that a County Fair "must offer three things – farming, youth and action, but that agriculture comes first because farming was the genesis of the Fair, and continues to be the principal atmosphere…"

"We keep trying to find things for young people to keep them interested in the fair, with an eye to the future when they will be persons who bring their children back to compete."

The Fair now heralded itself as "the Fair with the flair for the future." An increasing number of celebrities began to visit – Miss America, Miss Canada and John Fairfax, the 32-year-old Briton who was the first man to row across the Atlantic alone, were among them - apparently they thought so too.

END of 1960's

Eden Corn Festival float at the Fair

America's County Fair
Chapter 14

The Erie County Fair reached its pinnacle in the 1970s. The long road from its seat on lands still bearing the stumps of trees failed to build shelter for the pioneers – through the years when bad weather cut the gate; past the innumerable risks taken to expand; the mortgages, the loans and above all the vision and determination to excel – climaxed in the decade the United States marked the Bicentennial.

At the 80th annual convention of the International Association of Fairs and Expositions at Chicago December 1, 1970, the Buffalo News reported

"California may be ahead of New York in population, but those concerned with the quality of life, rather than quantity, can give the Empire State a new "first" today."

"The Erie County Fair now is rated the biggest county fair in the country, passing the Los Angeles County Fair in Pomona, California, the leader for many years."

"The Fair reached the top spot with a 1970 attendance mark of 600,960."

People Enjoying Themselves at the Park

1970's

Arthur Godfrey enjoying the music of the Clayt Fattey band in Slade Park 1974

Added the Buffalo Courier Express: "The County Fair is far larger than many state fairs…and last year (1969) surpassed the crowds at the New York State Fair in Syracuse… The Erie County Agricultural Society is the oldest non-profit, industrial and commercial organization in the county."

It was in the 1970s, in 1979 to be exact, that an extra day was added to the Fair's run, establishing a 10-day schedule which has continued ever since.

In 1976, admission price was raised from $1 to $2 for all fairgoers over 12 years. The layout of the fairgrounds was impressive. On 260 acres now stood 70 buildings sheltering interests ranging from livestock to machinery, from educational outreach to entertainment – all set on land developed to provide attractive and convenient area for resting, dining, picnicing, and not to mention parking; 30,000 cars could now be accommodate

A long way from the rows of farm wagons and buggies that crowded the fences of the old Fair 100 years before.

Parking was free until 1979, when labor costs for attendants caused a charge of $1 per car.

It seems fitting now to speak of those centers of shade and relaxation for visitors to the Erie County Fair – the parks. Strategically and carefully planned over a half century, they now formed oasis of greenness and comfort throughout the grounds:

1970's

*Slade Park, named after Frank A Slade, long-time Society Treasurer, was formerly swampland. It was established in the early 1920s as an old-fashioned village park with a bandstand, and lit by gas lamps. It is now bright with flowerbeds.

*Arthur G. Fries Park, honoring the former Director of Conservation, has a large illuminated fountain with a 15-foot jet as its centerpiece.

*Baker Park, a salute to Dr. Harrison V. Baker, who for several decades directed the harness racing program at the track, features unusual shrubs as well as flower beds.

* Hickory Park Picnic Grove set out in 1970, a four-acre area wooded mostly by hickory trees. Inviting picnic tables, benches and grills stand beneath them. "It's all in the interest of economy for the fair visitors," wrote Sue Buyer of the Buffalo Evening News.

*Howdy Doody Shows'
1973*

*Clarabell and Buffalo Bob Smith
at the Erie County Fair*

1970's

The Keystone Cops take a break in Slade Park 1975

The 200 rose bushes planted along the fence of the fairgrounds now form a glorious red barricade in season. Trees of various species replace those lost to the Dutch Elm disease, so devastating in Western New York.

New plans and actualities characterized the Fair in the 1970s. "By maintaining its policy of annual improvement, the Erie County Fair and Exposition offers its patrons one of the most luxurious settings to be found in any of the nation's fairgrounds," reported the Buffalo Courier-Express, at the opening of the 1972 Fair.

"The new livestock buildings eliminated the need for tents."

1970's

MARGARET LOCKWOOD

"The new Youth Livestock Building will house 4-H and FFA beef and dairy cattle. The building is 70-x-200 feet, and is designed to accommodate more than 200 animals that will be exhibited by over 100 Erie County youngsters.

"The new Open Class Beef Cattle Building, 70-x-140 feet in size, houses 140 head of beef cattle. The beef cattle will be exhibited by many of New York State's largest beef farms. The total cost of the building is approximately $100,000.

The gigantic Health Services Building, (oldest building on the fairgrounds), one of the few remaining octagon-shaped buildings in existence in Western New York was completely renovated and improved last year. The public will be given the opportunity to take advantage of the free diagnostic clinics offered by the various health services in the county."

In 1975 the Women's Department proudly moved into its new building called the Creative Arts Building on the gala Avenue of Flags.

Overflowing success prompted the interesting sociological development of a marked increase in interest of men in crafts, fine arts and photography at the Fair.

Commented Mrs. Clarence N. Lockwood, Secretary of the Women's Board for more than 30 years, and perhaps the grand matriarch of the Fair: "Creative Arts seemed to include anyone interested in Household Accessories, Fine Arts or the Flower Show. It has worked out well, and we do have many men as well as a large Junior Department."

Octagon Building
Oldest Standing Building on Fairgrounds

1970's

*Flower Display
at the
Creative Arts Building*

The spirit of women, who nearly a century before strove for stature in the Society, must have smiled gently as they officially received with grace "the stronger sex" into their ranks in the late 20th century.

Cherished by exhibitors in the Creative Arts division is the TriColor Award, an honorary award chosen by the judge for the outstanding article among those entered in competition in each section. The Award of Distinction, chosen by the Department's Directors from the sectional TriColor winners, is its "Best of Show" prize. An invitation only outdoor luncheon, is the annual social highlight of the Creative Arts Department.

As attendance at the Fair increased, more water facilities were required. A $200,000 sewage system, the largest single project yet built on the grounds, was installed in 1975.

A new roadway was laid on the west side of the fairgrounds, from the back of the Agriculture and Grange Building to the back of the Firemen's Building in 1978. It was humorously named "42nd Street" after New York City's famous thoroughfare, in expectation of heavy traffic along it.

Society, not to be outdone by the metropolis, celebrated the opening with dancing in a tent along the road, to the strains of Woody Herman and his band. There was disco dancing under the two new domes that rose on the grounds as the '70s closed.

"The two structures, purchased from the National Aeronautics and Space Administration…were formerly used by the Smithsonian Institution and Cape Canaveral," announced the Buffalo Courier-Express. "The domes, made from tubular steel and covered with vinyl canvases, measure 120 feet in diameter and 30 feet high."

"One of the domes will house exhibits behind the grandstand near the conservation area. The other will be a musical showcase for pop music stars, groups, and disco dancing."

Tommy Dorsey and Jimmy Dorsey's orchestras played, and pop singing star Bobby Vinton and the Statler Brothers sang at the Fair in 1979. Each of these groups would have been the major attraction at any national event.

But the greatest aesthetic feather in a Society's cap was the arrival of Richard Huntington, art critic of the Buffalo Courier-Express, at the Creative Arts Building at the final fair of the '70s. As with the appearance of the Buffalo Philharmonic Orchestra at the Fair for the first time in 1955, it was a cultural highmark. Drama critics too, reviewed Fair entertainment.

The new deluxe clubhouse was of prime interest. With an overall capacity of 2,000, the air-conditioned facility enclosed a parquet circle on the second floor for dining, enabling 150 fairgoers to see events on the race track, the grandstand stage or in the infield's Home Show arena. An adjacent room accommodated 850 diners, the cocktail lounge 275 guests.

The grandstands also were renovated bringing the total capacity, combined with the clubhouse, to 10,000.

Notable too, was the increase in sponsoring groups and their tie-in with the Fair. For example, in 1979 there was Shrine Day, Grange-Kiwanis Day, Buffalo-Firemen's Day, Demo Derby Day (billed as the world's largest demolition derby), and Senior Citizen's Day. Skillfully, the organizational ranks of the County were interwoven more and more with Fair activities.

Judges of the horse show, now offering more than 600 classes, came increasingly long distances to officiate at the Erie County Fair.

Despite a changing world around it, the Erie County Agricultural Society has endeavored down the years to be loyal to one intrinsic purpose. As its founders, those stalwart Yankee and German farmers declared at its formal establishment in 1856:

"The business and object of said Society shall be the promotion of the Agricultural, Historical, Mechanical and Manufacturing interests of said county."

It is a purpose tenaciously held to and stated in the midst of dwindling farm population, a revolution in transportation and communications, and the plethora of entertainment available to a fun-loving American people.

With the ability to engage or hire top national entertainers and high-powered Midway amusements; with strong ties to state and county health and educational agencies and area cultural groups —

Arthur Godfrey with "Goldie" appearance in 1974

1970's

131

Delighted by the Scrambler

Society in 1970 still proclaimed its loyalty to the Earth, its produce and livestock, the scientific advances that improve them, and the homelife of those who make this possible.

But the issue was discussed. Speaking after the 1974 Fair when attendance topped the previous year by nearly 10,000. Fair Manager Benjamin DeYoung Jr. said: "We try to have something for everyone."

Of the needs for a successful fair, he said the most important thing was "direct competition, as in the sprint car races, horse and pony pulls and demolition derbies."

"While it is important to have good entertainment, the star stuff is foolish," he said. "Having big name stars doesn't necessarily mean you are going to have a successful fair. More people would prefer to see Aunt Anna's prize-winning rug or their children's 4-H winners."

Yet, in truth, they wanted and were given both.

In 1976, George G. Sipprell, a member of the board for 28 years and now Treasurer, said he was basically satisfied with the Fair's present and longstanding mix of farm-related and midway entertainment.

But while the midway gives the Fair some income through rental space to concessionaires, Mr. Sipprell emphasized that farm-oriented activities must remain at center stage.

"We've got to maintain as much of the past as possible..." he told the Buffalo Courier-Express. "Erie County still has a large amount of acreage devoted to farming." The Buffalo Evening News reported that Society, at its annual meeting in preparation for the 139th Fair in 1978, again renewed its loyalty to its nomenclature by determining "to renew its commitment to promoting agriculture." Treasurer Sipprell also said that plans for a $500,000 livestock exhibition center would start that year.

Paul Laing, Secretary of the Fair, commented on the agricultural exhibit situation as the Country's economy lagged:

1970's

"Our basic purpose is to promote agriculture. It is the backbone of the Fair. This year we have a farm implement show, a free farming booklet handout and of course, the exhibits plus a demonstration.

"If the exhibits are down it is because of the cost. Farmers are struggling to stay alive. Many simply can't afford the time or money for a week's stay at the fair."

The change in farm population was reflected in both animal and bird exhibits.

Mrs. Vi Ehlers of Orchard Park, who for 25 years had recorded entries in the rabbit, poultry and pigeon department, expressed it: "Very few are farmers," she said. "Most raise these animals and birds as a hobby, including many young people in the last few years. There were so few entries in the egg laying contest this year we didn't have it."

The produce department also reflected the change: "In the agriculture building, the produce exhibits are beginning to come in…" reported the press. "They are firm red tomatoes with flawless skins, bright green celery with a profusion of leaves, stick straight cucumber pickles and dusky red, round beets.

"A commercial farmer could not afford to grow and harvest such specimens. Most are the result of backyard specialized gardeners with the time to nature perfection."

But farm or backyard gardener exhibiting at the Fair – the ranks of this old, growing, successful institution continued to expand with spread-eagle vigor.

It survived a major encounter with the Town of Hamburg in the '70s. Hamburg claimed Society, a non-profit organization, should pay a tax on its property, assessed at $1.8 million, because it leased 52 acres of its grounds to the profit making Buffalo Raceway.

Court action ensued, but New York States' highest court, the Court of Appeals, ruled the exemption should stand, on grounds that state law specifically exempts Agricultural Societies from taxes – no matter how the property is used.

Produce Display

1970's

133

Nostalgia has long been an integral part of the Fair. A Society that has spanned a-century-and-a-half has naturally gathered much respect for and loyalty to the past.

The Fair, long a stamping ground of patriotism, celebrated the Bicentennial in style.

"This, after all, is the only Bicentennial year we will ever have," heralded the Buffalo Courier-Express.

"And in honor of that, the fairgrounds' broad avenue of Flags is adorned this year, not with flags from each of the states, but rather 50 identical, 13 star Betsy Ross style American flags."

Heritage Hall, just off the midway, offered an exhibit in 1976 of memorabilia of past fairs, including photographs, equine publications and glass-topped cases of ribbons, certificates and premium lists.

Built by the Indians themselves in the original manner, without aid of modern tools, its longhouse, burial grounds, stockade and other structures indigenous to such settlements held perhaps the greatest mystique of any display at the Fair – a centuries old tie with the Western New York of the past. Shows, lectures and crafts were offered.

A time capsule was buried on the fairgrounds at the Bicentennial to be opened in 2076. Enclosed was a $500 bond, as a "symbol of faith in the future of America," and a letter to Society's Board of Directors of 2076 recommending that the future proceeds, worth "at least $60,000," at current rate of interest, be used for agricultural scholarships and ground improvements. (Even in the distance of time Society held close to the earth.) Other deposits included a history of the

Blase Pasquarella, Art Freeze, Clayt Taylor and Earl Henry prepare to bury the time capsule in the front lawn of the Historical Building 1976

1970's

1970's

Society, newspapers, premium books, and additional memorabilia.

But the span of life as we know it today happens at the Fair. Shirley Farley's cow gave birth to a calf early in the week at the 1970 Fair. Resting in their stall until the fair was about to close, mother and child were led out to begin the long trek home to Geneseo in Livingston County.

Ledgewood Comet, a Morgan gelding 23 years old owned by Mr. and Mrs. James S. Burghduff of Snyder had been shown at the fair for 18 years. He was a favorite of local horse lovers.

"After winning the last of what is described as a 'basketful of ribbons,' Corky, as he is known to his numerous friends, was retired in moving ceremonies at the center of the horse ring," reported the press on August 25, 1974.

"Tears ran down Mrs. Burghduff's face as Corky's long-time rider, Mrs. Phyllis Whitchurch of Clarence Center dismounted to let the Burghduff's daughter,

Mark Leitzan
Horse Show in Front of Grandstand
1972

Sharing Stories with the Fairgoer

Wende, ride Corkey out of the arena to the applause of hundreds of admirers."

The Erie County Horse Show which this fine chestnut horse had graced so long was now known as one of the most prestigious showing fields in the country; as the '70s drew to a close, it was drawing 1,000 entries.

4-H, "Head, Heart, Hands and Health" – the youth program of the Cornell Cooperative Extension Service, has long flourished in Erie County. Open to boys and girls between 8 to 19 years of age of all races and religious faiths, it originally was a rural-based endeavor, which now has spread to the city (38%) and the suburbs (48%), leaving only 14% in the dwindling rural areas.

But today it thrives, with more than 20,000 members engaged in over 500 projects, led by more than 850 volunteers.

The Erie County Agricultural Society has long fostered and supported 4-H as an incubator and promoter of farm and home interests, as well as youth development.

Success of the Fair in 4-H activities is reflected in a report by the Buffalo Courier-Express at the 1978 Fair:

The 4-H program, always a vital part of this County's Fair, will get into full swing on the second day with the judging beginning at 10 a.m. The grand champion steer and 80 other blue, red and white ribbon winners will go up for public auction at 8 p.m.

The program provides discipline for the young potential farmer to the hard realities of agriculture - cultivating the soil, producing crops and the raising of livestock. Hardest of all for the youth who have raised, trained and lived with a steer, cow, a hog or a sheep. Heartmoving good-byes are the climax of County Fairs. "Because of the number of market pigs raised by 4-H club members a few years back, exhibitors were told they could enter only one, not three pigs as in the past. Now the number of exhibitors has grown so, even with one hog apiece, there'll be a near-record of the 120 pigs to be judged Tuesday and sold Thursday.

"The 70 lambs raised by 4-H members also to be judged Tuesday, will be sold in an auction at 1:30 p.m. Thursday. The pig auction will follow."

Among other 4-H highlights at the Fair was their horse show and dog show, the latter featuring a costumed dog competition. But the Erie County Fair now offered a wider vista than field and barn, high action competition and increasingly sophisticated entertainment.

It extended contact with individuals and groups from around the world. Seeing a television performance can never excel seeing performers face to face. They bring their environment and personality to the viewer with far greater impact than is ever transmitted by the TV screen.

For example in 1976, the fairgrounds rang with the sound of the 140-member orchestra and chorus from Buffalo's Sister City, Kanazawa, Japan. Eighty crewmembers of the Norwegian tall ship Christian Radich, also were guests. Fairgoers, who might never see such groups and figures even on TV, had a firsthand glimpse of the international, the talented and the famous. The impact of such an encounter was particularly strong in the rural areas.

In addition, solid, practical information was handed out to the public: "In keeping with the public interest, the fair will include a voter informa-

1970's

tion booth to be manned by the Erie County Board of Elections," reported the press.

Again, "Fairgoers interested in good health can stop at the Health Building on the Avenue of Flags for blood pressure, diabetes, posture and mouth tests. Medical technicians also will weigh visitors and help them determine whether they are candidates for heart attacks."

"Literature is available on mental illness, alcoholism, old age, and a variety of other health problems and health and social agencies."

The scope of offerings at the Erie County Fair in the 1970s is reflected by just a few of the listings at the 139th Fair in 1978. They included "Bobbin lace making and macramé demonstrations in the Historical Building…Square dancing at the Outdoor Theater…every half hour farm animal demonstrations, including sheep shearing and goat milking in the Conservation Building…the Burger King Magic Show…Kin Tora Judo Club at Slade Park, and competing for sound was the Demolition Derby and Woody Herman and His Thundering Herd.

The Kramner Memorial Trophy, awarded each year to the outstanding pig exhibitor chosen by vote by his fellow exhibitors, went to David Becher of Collins. And a team driven by Charlie Kidd of Unity, Ohio won the heavy weight horse pull. The team pulled 3,750 pounds 23.7 feet.

Old time songs by the Statler Brothers surged over the grounds at the 140th Erie County Fair in 1979, as it closed with record attendance.

End of 1970's

Glenn Campbell 1973

138   1970's

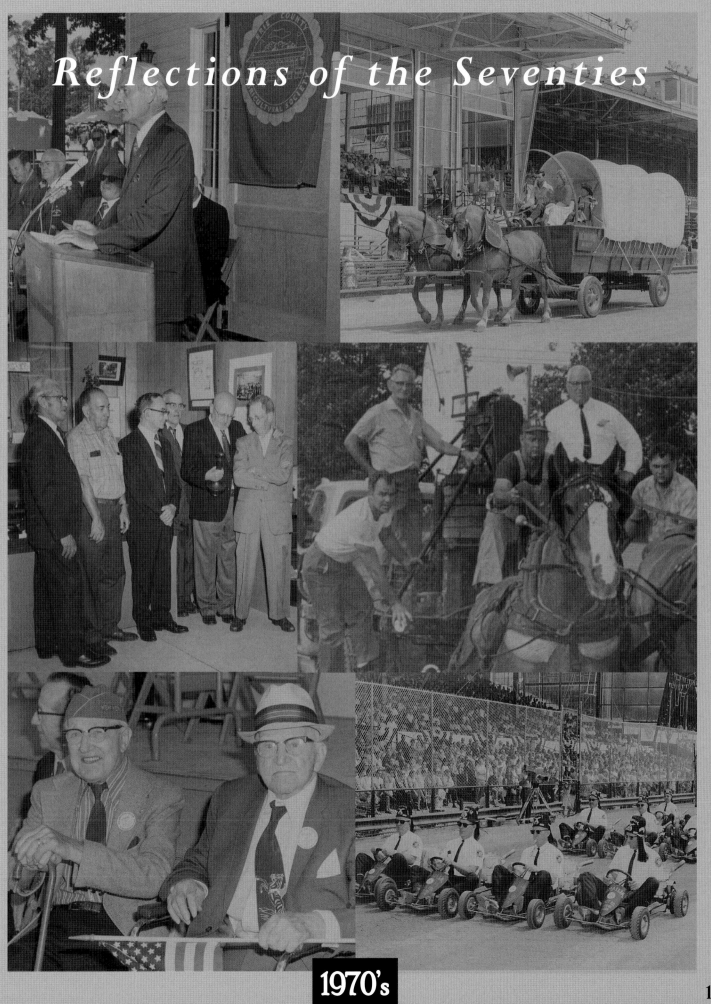

Reflections of the Seventies

1970's

"Tall oaks from little acorns grow..."
David Everett

Making a Difference
Chapter 15

North American 6-Horse Hitch Classic

Evolution of the Fair – from its foundering start in 1820 to its revival in 1842 to its Sesquicentennial in 1989 – has been marked by the perception and careful planning of those who organized and managed it. Its two dusty and windy days at Dr. Johnson's property on Delaware Avenue brought in receipts of about $500 from an estimated 2,000 persons.

The Sesquicentennial Fair was held for ten days on the 260 sprawling acres of the Hamburg Fairgrounds, with its 85 buildings, a race track, 7,000 seat grandstand and handsome clubhouse, drew receipts of $2,844,443 from a record crowd of 751,000.

In this interim of a century and a half, the United States moved from horseback and stagecoach to train and plane; from musket to atomic bomb; from Wells Fargo to United Parcel Services, and from quill pen to computer.

1980's

How has the Erie County Agricultural Society matched its wits and strengths with such tremendous changes and come out successfully?

Perhaps the simplistic answer is "We are flexible!" but there is more to it than that.

The Society was rooted in pioneer stock – a good start in any life – hardy New Englanders and stalwart Germans who formed an organization that began when the stumps of trees, felled to build shelter in Western New York, still ringed county pastures.

The Erie County Agricultural Society Fathers were thrifty; if there was a little leftover old lumber they disposed of it, whatever it was worth to each other or outsiders. They were good bargainers; they watched the till.

But they were ambitious; they wanted to "grow big." They had a vision and were willing to take chances to actualize it.

The same sense of adventure and drive that brought them to Western New York sustained them and their descendants in it.

Above all – they moved with the times.

The effect of the Fair on Erie County has been enormous. "It is good for local businesses too," reported the publication Business First in 1987. "The fair itself receives no money from the County and is a non-profit corporation. It usually takes in a maximum of only $250,000 a year, money that is put toward the upkeep and renovation of the grounds. But the fair does have an impact for County businesses estimated at $35 million." Even as the economy dipped, the Fair seemed able to hold its own:

"Even with Western New York's depressed economy and a host of new competing amusement parks in the area, people are still flocking, sometimes in record numbers, to America's largest County Fair," reported the Buffalo Courier-Express in August 1981. In 1983 with a record attendance of 614,277, the Fair brought in $2.04 million, achieving a surplus for the first time in three years.

Gross sales of $2,057,385 were reported at the 1985 Fair, atoning for a loss of $70,000 in 1984. And even when liability insurance for the 1986 Fair rose 300 percent, General Manager Paul C. Laing said, "We'll be able to give the public rides and thrills they've had in past years, plus some new ones. "We are one of the lucky ones.

The show will go on."

Aside from booking the latest entertainment acts through national agents, Laing, a natural "idea man" himself, visited 17 New York Fairs in 1987 to keep abreast of what others were doing and aware of new development and trends.

"He is always on top of things and a few steps ahead of other fairs," said Lloyd L. Lamb, second Vice-President. "Sometimes you'll go to conferences and they're trying to see what to do to better the fair, and you'll think, 'This fair has already done that!'"

In the face of a shrinking farm population and increasingly socially sophisticated times, the 150-year-old Erie County Agricultural Society has survived by braiding the interests of farm and city, and offering exhibits and contests

Robert W. Dygert D.V.M
Director

Ben De Young,
Past Manager

Paul C. Laing
Fair Manager

1980's

143

AGRI-CENTER
GROUND BREAKING
DECEMBER 13, 1989

1980's

that tap the root of public interest in either area:

"The reorganized Agricultural Society remains dedicated to promoting 'agricultural, horticultural, mechanical and manufacturing interests' (as it was constituted to do in 1856)," wrote Bob Buyer, longtime farm reporter for the Buffalo News, on the eve of the Fair's 150th year. "But the fair today is as much a showcase for the arts, food, cooking, history, youth development, merchandising and entertainment as it is for cattle, poultry, flowers, fruits and vegetables."

In December 1986, at its annual meeting, Society issued an announcement that bore witness to this braiding of interests and illustrated their foresight, flexibility and ability to move with the times:

"Building an Agri-Center on the Erie County Fairgrounds and creating a structure where shows, sales, exhibitions and other events can be staged 365 days of a year was a major initiative to emerge from this week's annual meeting of the Erie County Agricultural Society," announced the Buffalo News.

"The 1986 Directors of Erie County's oldest continuous organization aim to extend and expand its services by attracting small and large groups in and out of agriculture from Western New York and Southern Ontario."

"With more than an acre of indoor space, the Agri-Center would be a likely place to hold horse shows, livestock sales and shows as well as gatherings of smaller local groups…"

The press also pointed out that the Erie County Fair "didn't get where it is by mere momentum." As an example of aforementioned forethought, plans for the new center included large doors. "We want to be able to get anything in and out of the Agri-Center," noted Secretary Laing.

The Erie County Fair and Exposition was already a huge operation before it considered expansion.

Administration, logistics and harmonizing of an endeavor that embraces homo sapiens, animals and birds, yes, fish too, is not merely a challenge. It must be a tour de force. The alternative would be bedlam.

"It costs $1.3 million just to open the gates at the Fair," noted Paul Laing in 1982, as Society reported a direct payroll of $381,000 in connection with the operation. Of this — bearing out the value of the fair to the area — 44.5 percent was paid to Town of Hamburg

1980's

145

residents, and 70 percent to residents within a 5-mile radius.

The Society's payroll also included $33,500 for parking attendant services, and listed a $1,808,100 payroll for Buffalo Raceway and food services during the two racing seasons held at the fairgrounds. Payrolls of amusement ride operators and concessionaires were estimated at an additional $500,000. Approximately $2,722,650 was thus absorbed by Erie County's economy.

By 1987, a record 715,000 men, women and children had poured $2.25 million into Society's treasury at the Fair. Receipts for the remainder of the year from other sources totaled an additional $269,648, topping the previous five years intake.

Who were these visitors?

A survey of those attending the 147th Fair of the Erie County Agricultural Society showed 36.5 percent were between 40 and 59 years old, and 32.9 percent between 21 and 39 years. Of that audience, 19.5 percent were city dwellers, 40.7 lived in the suburbs, and 6.4 percent were from farms; the remainder were residents of small towns or rural areas.

Survey showed that 59.7 percent traveled up to 25 miles to attend the fair and 3.7 percent hailed from other states.

The low 6.4 percent of farm visitors to the Fair seemed to validate Society's plans for the new Agri-Center, which would help re-emphasize the Veterans organization's dedication to agriculture and provide funds for its accomplishment.

Open Class Color Breed Dairy Cattle

Where Fairgoers are able to get close to cows

The attention of the Fair is focused on a dwindling agricultural industry, which was stressed by Paul Laing: "We're the only people left to educate the people about agriculture," he told Business First of Buffalo in 1987. "No one out there has the time to devote to telling about agriculture. Ninety-six percent of those who attend the Fair are not in agriculture, even though it is the largest industry in New York."

"We want everyone to know where a glass of milk comes from," he said. "(It's) not from the supermarket."

146

1980's

To this end, an $18,000 milking parlor was built for use during the fair. The public can see where the milk comes from and farmers have a place to milk their cows."

During the Fair more than 3,000 people, including exhibitors and concessionaires, live on the fairgrounds. Then there are the thousands of daily visitors.

"It's like putting a city together," said Paul Laing. "We have all the problems a city has for 10 days, except we have animal waste and they don't."

There is also a question of temperament: "It's always a problem working with the superstars, and then there are some organizations that think they are the only ones in the Fair," he said. "The object is to try and blend a day's events (from grandstand shows to livestock judging in the barns) into something workable."

The next Fair is planned almost immediately after the last one. But when the time arrives, a lightning transformation must be made of the race track to convert it to Fair use. Fences surrounding the track must come down, and betting booths removed and replaced with concession stands. Racehorse stables are turned into barns to house show horses, cattle and sheep. It takes about 11 strenuous days.

Exhibit, Contest, Entertainment and Food, the age-old four-leaf-clover of the Erie County Fair and Exposition, grew and flourished as the Fair approached its Sesquicentennial in 1989.

Erie County farm owners who had survived and their descendants – with pardonable pride – must have smiled as they thought of the great Pan-American Exposition of 1901 in Buffalo, once so out doing the Fair's largely rural offerings.

Fundamentally based on the land itself and what it could yield, rather than on spectacle, the Fair, which started on horseback or with ox team, had survived the wonders and persuasions of a technological age.

Farm columnist Bob Buyer of the Buffalo News pointed this out in 1983:

"While this 144th edition (of the Fair), likely to be witnessed by more than a half a million persons, will hardly resemble the first one (1820)… it will still have been built around farm and home life and personal achievement."

In the 1980s, exhibits embraced a spectrum ranging from Seneca Indians Neville and Juanita Springs' display of Northeast Indian silver earrings, pendants, medallions and pins they designed in 1983, which allegedly reflected influence by Europeans who traded with the Indians in the late 1600s – to an exhibit from the Encyclopedia Britannica's collection of life-sized statues of famous native American chiefs, complete with commentary on their lives and exploits. The Fair also displayed the noted home library at three locations.

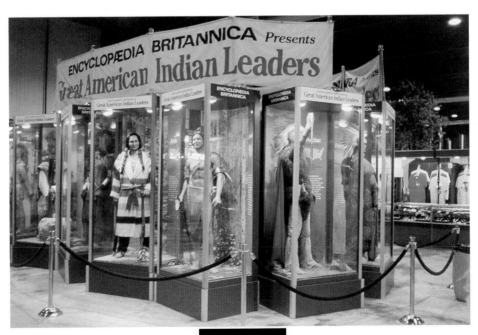

1980's

*Fairgoers root on their favorite rooster during
annual Rooster Crowing Contest*

Then always alert to national presentations, a miniature museum rolled into the fairgrounds in 1984, honoring the 100th anniversary of Eleanor Roosevelt's birth and depicting her life story.

Frederick R. Skrabucha of West Seneca gave a turkey-calling demonstration, a bird whose wild population had been renewed by state conservationists to an estimated 40,000.

Far, far from the days of the tin Saturday night tub and the farm pond, the Mini-Mall of 1986 offered the latest in whirlpool bathtubs, spas (for two or more people); and the replacement of the cast iron skillet of yore by an egg-frying demonstration in a non-stick pan and new rug cleaners mocking old wicker carpet beaters.

Contest: Lording over his elders, a bull calf owned by Marvin Luders of Elma was chosen as the grand champion bull of Western New York Regional Holstein Show in 1983, as a small Silver Duckwing rooster, from the coops of Rick Martinez of Blasdell crowed 45 times in 15 minutes to set a record and win the annual Rooster Crowing Contest at the Fair. Roosters were not the only ones who exulted in sound there; a cheerleading contest was held in 1984 at the infield bleacher.

A 1983 strike for the feminist image was made when four young women placed first in every class of the cattle-showing competition.

1980's

"The girls were noticeably better in handling their animals (15 to 17-month-old, 1,000-to-1,300 pound bovines)" said Judge Peter Comerford.

There was nearly every conceivable type of race for human to animal participants. The 10-kilometer run sponsored by the National Kidney Foundation in which overall winner Mark D. Hume, 22, of East Aurora, triumphed over 400 male and female runners with a time of 31.19; the popular "Dash for the Mash" in which trained pigs sprint around a eighth-of-a mile track to a savory mash at its finish, and by the decade's close, goat and duck races too.

The interest and delight in the demonstration of horsepower — animal or tractor — was fully satisfied in the 1980s. The latter event was significant evidence of the farm community's acceptance of the machine age, and indeed of its awestruck wonder at it. Light weight horse teams, splendid Belgians or Percherons, weighing up to 3,200 pounds, and heavyweights, sometimes as much as 4,500 pounds, enthralled large audiences with exhibits of pulling weighted trucks beyond human strength for $8,000 in prize money.

In 1987 Francis Root of Bolivar captured the $1,000 first prize with his team pulling a 4,225-pound load a distance of 27.5 feet. But the fine gallant teams were not sufficient for an avid public in a modern age. By 1986 "bull" tractors joined the ranks of heavyweights.

"Tractor pulling, once the sole domain of the farmer, has taken on some new and loud dimensions at county fairs and

The Erie County Fair Marching Band
is made up of approximately 100
Juniors and Seniors
from
Western New York High Schools

1980's

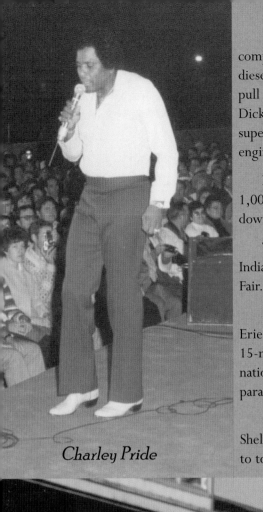

Charley Pride

competitions throughout the United States," reported the Buffalo News in 1983. "The diesel fuel and alcohol-eating monsters will be taking the track… to decide who can pull the most weight in the fastest time at the 144th Annual Erie County Fair… Tom Dickerson of Olean will be in the 7,000-pound superstock competition tonight. The superstocks are regular farm tractors that have been "souped-up" by turbocharging and engine modification.

Dickerson's high-powered International Harvester 686 tractor now generates over 1,000 horsepower and takes the 300-foot pull in approximately 15 seconds, sucking down 3 gallons of diesel fuel."

The National Tractor Association was sponsored in 1985 and pullers from Ohio, Indiana, Illinois, North Carolina and Pennsylvania joined 17 New York teams at the Fair.

Entertainment: Nationally famous singing stars and bands continued to visit the Erie County Fair in the 1980s. But there were also area favorites, like Clayton Fattey's 15-member Band, a tradition at the Fair since 1927, opening the event with the national anthem, and the 120-piece Erie County Fair Marching Band, a harmonizer of parades and spectacles.

Charlie Pride with his hit "Kiss an Angel Good Morning,"… Country music stars Shelly West, David Frizzell, Louise Mandrell, Boxcar Willie, the Texas Trainmen, and to top it all off again the Statler Brothers in 1983, followed by the Country Music

Chrystal Gayle

1980's

VFW Pvt. Leonard Post on parade route 1982

Association's 1984 top male vocalist Lee Greenwood and his predecessor as entertainer of the year, Ronnie Milsap. By 1986 Willie Nelson was singing "All the Girls I've Loved" at the Fair.

Bands inspired and swayed Fair visitors with tunes that satisfied the "Now" generation, or took older men and women back to the '40s and '50s on the domed dance floor:

Charley Daniels Band, the Nitty Gritty Dirt Band, Mike Mulawka's Swing Orchestra, and Tommy Dorsey's Band and Glenn Miller's Orchestra for dancing.

Veterans' bands brought something beyond entertainment to the Fair. At the annual Veterans' Day parade on the eve of the Sesquicentennial, about 15,000 marchers in 87 units drew a crowd of 123,395 spectators, the largest attendance in the Fair's history.

Joe Solomon placing wreath on Veteran's Memorial

TO ALL VETERANS OF ALL WARS
AUGUST 16, 1981
ERIE COUNTY AGRICULTURAL SOCIETY

1980's

The veterans' units and their auxiliaries were resplendent in costume and paraphernalia — "The parade was a river of bugles, bagpipes, helmets and batons," wrote the Buffalo Evening News.

1980's

News, "brought more pomp and circumstance to the Fair." They brought memories of the six wars the Fair had lived through and echoes of a former seventh, the War of 1812, as the parade passed by. They tied the past of area families to the present; marching memorials, they symbolized the glory and heartache of war.

"We're getting more and more participants from outside Erie County," said Bob Harris, parade coordinator. "We've got every American war represented here, not the Civil War of course, but we have a re-enactment of that war in the parade."

There was the Midway. A ribbon cutting ceremony took place in 1984 celebrating the 60th anniversary of the James E. Strates Shows at the Fair.

The Strates Shows, North America's largest carnival, by the 1980s carried a troupe of more than 1,000 food vendors, ride operators and technicians as it rolled annually into Hamburg in 60 railroad cars and

1980's

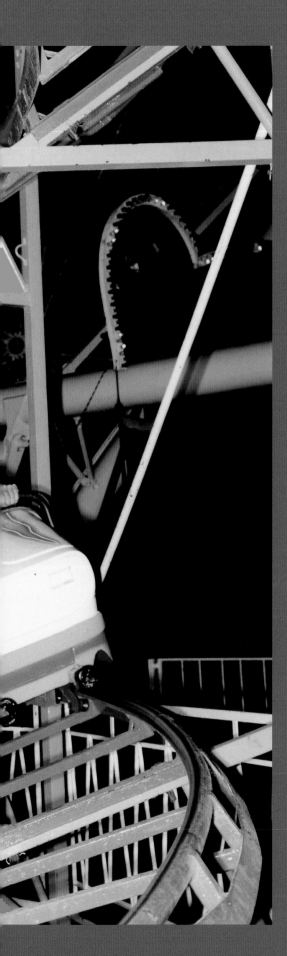

24 semi-trailers on its way to fairs from New England to Florida.

Dapper Benjamin Braunstein, 80, public relations man for the show, who had been with it for 63 years since its founding in

1923, says "I've watched this business grow from a little truck show to a multimillion dollar operation with state-of-the-art equipment. I'd never trade it!"

At the 1985 Fair, Strates Shows, with its 100 carnival games, introduced the sensational $250,000 Thunderbolt Ride, which joined the popular 166-foot-long Wild River Flume Ride, one of only two in the United States, and the 90-foot-high Rainbow Ride, a German importation.

Every coin has two sides. It might well be said that the Strates Shows today, are the other side of the coin at the great Erie County Fair.

1980's

Food: The activity of the Fair promotes appetite, and food has long been its mainstay. The volume and variety of nourishment served to the crowd of thousands each year is staggering - it's also big business.

Leonard J. Coffey, Concession Manager of the Fair, noted that professionally run food concessions have all but replaced the local volunteer-run church or fraternal lodge stands designed to raise money for their organizations. Luscious pies offered by such groups are cherished memories of Fair old-timers.

H.B. Leonard, a concessionaire for 27 years, who runs a cotton candy booth there, the most nostalgic of fair offerings said, "It's only water and sugar, but people seem to like it more than anything else." His next best sellers were candied apples. Mr. Leonard expected an $800-a-day return at the 1983 Fair.

A Pasta House stand looked for 10,000 customers, while Thomas P. Chiavetta, operator of a chicken restaurant for 29 years, predicted that at least 30,000 would eat Fair chicken dinners.

Sy Kolassa, a Fair vendor for more than a quarter-of-a-century, admits no one has ever weighed the food consumed during an Erie County Fair run, but assures that literally "tons of taffy and fudge" will be sold.

Society kept a smart eye on the merchandising of the Fair, endeavoring, as the economy flagged, to strike a balance between increasing production costs and the public purse, compromising when necessary.

In the Spring of 1982, a single ticket was launched - $7 at the gate or $6 if pre-purchased. It would entitle visitors from 5 years old and up to general admission, a grandstand seat for any show and tickets to every Midway ride and show. The "walk-around" ticket or general admission however, rose from $2.50 to $4.00.

Formerly, general admission, grandstand seats and rides or shows tickets were purchased separately and cost much more. But with the new "Super Ticket," as it was called, attendance at the 1982 Fair dropped 5 percent. The new venture was abandoned at year's end. Gate admission in 1983 was set at $3.50 for adults and $2 for senior citizens and children under 12 years. Advance tickets for adults were $2.50.

A survey by management major students at Canisius College approved of the price change. Interview of 201 persons in the northern part of the County, where attendance was less than the south, showed that people did not like having to buy a ticket that covered everything. Under a reverse plan - $3.50 for adults or $2.50 in advance, and $2.00 for senior citizens or $1.75 in advance — attendance at the 1983

1980's

Fair rose 36,550 above the previous years.

Flexibility by Society again paid off. By 1985, the Fair broke all records with a crowd of 695,275, nearly 75,000 above the year before. An informal survey by the Buffalo News in 1988 estimated the cost of taking a family of four to the Fair was $50 – admission $15, food $15, and rides $20. Few games however, cost less than $1.00. Most days an all-ride Midway ticket costs $7.50.

Unresting on its laurels, the Fair continued its march of progress as it approached its 150th anniversary.

For example, in 1983 Society was first in New York State to establish the only double track for the popular tractor pull. Communications were stepped up. Visitors to the Southtowns Radio Association's booth could send 20-word messages to anyone anywhere in the United States. A ten-minute slide show of the Fair, narrated by WBEN radio sports announcer Van Miller, was made available to clubs and organizations.

But the big news was that by 1985, the Fair had its own television program, and before the decade was out appeared in an hour-long special on cable TV's TNN – The Nashville Network.

1980's

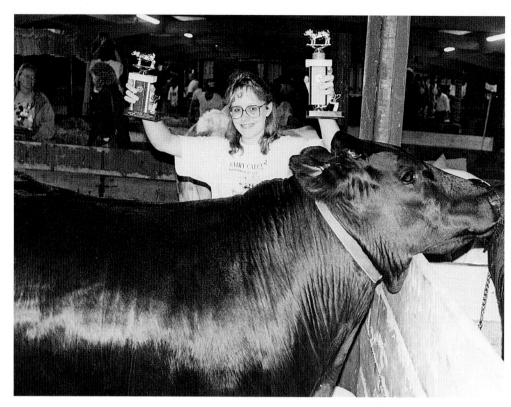

Jessica Gominiak proudly showing off her Master Showman trophies.

Jessica became the Agricultural Manager of the Fair in 1999.

"We're trying to show a side other than the Midway," a TNN representative said, " fairs for 2,000 years have provided an opportunity for local people to bring their best livestock and produce, the best products of their hands and skill, to show their neighbors."

It was the first time TNN had gone to a Fair, and the producers picked Erie County Fair and Exposition and the Walworth County Fair in Wisconsin as the best examples of what's good about Fairs.

A new building for the Oktoberfest celebration was added in 1985 too. The Youth Building was refurbished with a well-appointed kitchen for 4-Hrs.

While the Fair itself – from livestock to art exhibits – is educational, new instructional features were continually added like a ski demonstration; a 36-foot plastic ramp set at a 15-degree angle and covered with a mixture of water and detergent, simulating a snowy slope. It was manned by certified skiing instructors from Kissing Bridge Ski School. The demonstration was free and equipment provided.

The contribution to all Americans by the development of aviation was depicted in a slide show in the domed-air-conditioned theater in 1986. The Buffalo Police Department presented a puppet show on the dangers of drugs.

Strong ties between the Fair and the business community of the region illustrated the value of each to one another, lessening the gap between merchant and farmer.

Banks, supermarkets, brewers, soft drink bottlers, auto agencies all joined Society as sponsors of the Fair, forming a mutually rewarding meshwork, an acknowledgement of the changing demography of today's Society.

Tradition and loyalty personified walked the flower-bordered pathways of the Erie County Fair in the 1980s. None are more memorable than its Treasurer and Historian George G. Sipprell who in 1980 celebrated 32 years service to the Fair, a moving force in its 20th Century development... there was Charles Rogers, 83, who with his wife, Nellie, 82, showed 27 cows raised on their Randolph dairy farm in 1983. "I've been showing cattle at the Erie County Fair for 50 years," he said smiling, "and I've got no intention of stopping now"... 21-year old Dean Emley who had been selling chocolate-covered frozen bananas for five years on the Midway, and planned to stick with it for years to come, "It's not for everybody, but I love it"... Walter T. Binkowski official bugler for the Fair's opening ceremony since 1974... a 70-year oldster, who displayed his freehand needlepoint design of the multispired Mormon Temple in Washington, and George H. Hebard Jr., an attorney and Fair Treasurer in 1988, who grew up near the fairgrounds and has been involved in the Fair since he hauled water for the carnival elephants as a child. They were all there.

And the age-old life of field and barn and sty and hutch and hive flowed on at the Erie County Fair.

Antique Farm Implement Display
A popular attraction to suburban fairgoers!

Agricultural Specialist Bruce Tillapaugh of the Cooperative Extension of Erie and Wyoming Counties spent all day judging his specialty – field and forage products, like wheat and rye.

"As for the prize money which is listed in the 1984 Premium List of the Erie County Fair & Expo…" reported the press. "There's little chance of retiring off the winnings. The first prize for eggplant, for example, is $4. The second place winner gets $3, and to the third-place winner goes $2.

"Then again, there is the priceless sense of pride in knowing that you have grown the best in the County."

Record prices were received for 4-H-member-grown lambs and pigs in 1985 - $9.25 per pound for the 113-pound grand champion lamb owned by Heidi Kelkenpberg of Clarence Center, an all-time, all-breed high. Paul Majewski of Eden's 235-pound grand champion pig went for $4.90 a pound.

Courtney Fitzpatrick posing with her sheep

1980's

Illustrative of the rise in prices, two years later a grand champion lamb raised by Cybil Robbins, 14, of Langford sold for $24 a pound, while Matthew Tadt, 14, of Collins, received $10.75 a pound for his grand champion pig.

But even wholesalers have hearts. Sorrento Cheese Co. of Buffalo, purchaser of Cybil Robbins' lamb, was so moved by her tears at parting from her long-tended charge that the lamb was returned to her.

Apiarist Freeland M. Blodgett of Batavia manned a display of a telephone booth-sized enclosure housing 70,000 honeybees – without a sting. Mr. Blodgett emphasized that pollination was more important than honey.

It should be noted here that with literally thousands of birds and beasts at the Fair vigilant medical surveillance is a must.

A group of 30 practicing Erie County Veterinarians are recruited annually to attend this varied population – which may range from a blue ribbon horse to a champion rabbit – during the ten days of the Fair's run.

Coordinated by Robert W. Dygert, DVM, and Kerry Washburn, DVM, the recruits serve without remuneration.

In lieu of such recompense, Society offers scholarships to be divided among three needy Veterinary students, in their junior or senior year at recognized Veterinary Schools in the country. Applicants must be residents of one of the seventy eight towns of Western New York.

Numerous other scholarships promoting the cause of agriculture have been given down the years.

With all its success, the Erie County Agricultural Society has remembered to give as well as receive.

In 1989 an Endowment Fund had been established for use in furthering the objectives of the Fair. Several Endowment Fund Awards are conferred for outstanding achievement in the Cattle, Creative Arts, Horse Pull and Horse Show Departments.

Society also offers $4,000 annually in scholarships to June high school graduates who are enrolled in Agricultural, Horticultural, Agri-Business, Forestry or Veterinary Medicine programs in accredited colleges. Applications are made through the schools' guidance counselor's offices.

In addition, there is the annual Fred E. and Ann R. Sparling Memorial Agricultural Scholarship of $2,500 offered to students of Akron High School, Akron, New York, for agricultural related studies. The fund is dispensed over a two-year period.

1980's

Newborn calf experiences it's first Fair

The Paul C. Laing Scholarship of $1,000 annually, with specifications as offered by Society to high school graduates, would be established in the future.

From the outset, the Erie County Agricultural Society has paid tribute to its deceased. Minutes of this long-standing assemblage record repeated testimonials to officers and members who have served the Fair —even "unto the third and fourth generation." Their accomplishments and character are recorded with heartfelt gratitude and appreciation.

A number of Memorials other than the parks, and the aforementioned Memorial include those to Presidents Paul A. Laing, Earl Lexo and Benjamin DeYoung.

The great days arrived August 11-20, 1989. The Erie County Agricultural Society: 150 years old.

Society supporters commemorated the occasion by building a new gate at the South Park Avenue entrance to the Fair, with bricks they paid for, a tribute to the past and a welcome to the future.

Not to be behind the times, the night before the opening, Society welcomed youth at a free grandstand concert honoring the 30th anniversary of Rock'n'Roll.

Slade Park was the scene of the official opening the next day. On Sunday, as usual, Church Service was held at the 42nd Street Music Dome, where special thanks were offered.

Sammy Kaye's Orchestra offered dancing in the Super Duper Music Dome.

Paul C. Laing
a.ka.
"Tractor Pull Laing"

Paul A. Lang
a.ka.
"Horse Pull Lang"

1980's

The 3,000 workers manned the 400 food and concession stands, more than 1,000, the non-food ones. Wilson Enterprises sold about 650 cups of lemonade at $1.50 a cup on a Sunday, 60 more at night.

A record 751,000 men, women and children thronged the 1989 Fair.

The traditional fireworks seemed particularly bright. The fireworks were supplied by Zambelli Internationale, creators of the Statue of Liberty Fireworks in New York Harbor in 1986.

How did it all happen? What made this long and adventurous venture of the Erie County Agricultural Society succeed? The answer seems to have been given 50 years ago — at Society's 100th birthday celebration. The forward in the Premium Book of August, 1940, says it all!

One hundred years, as man reckons time, is a long period. To have established, a century ago, a friendship and a spirit of loyalty and confidence which have been enhanced through the years is an achievement of which any organization may be proud. Just five score years ago the first Fair of the Erie County Agricultural Society was held. It was a small and unpretentious thing, but the motivating was sound. The men who promoted it were community leaders, as are those who promote the Erie County Fair today. They were actuated by a desire for the betterment of their neighbors and their neighbors' affairs — and the same desire prevails today.

1980's

163

Through the ten decades since that first small fair was held, progress has been the guiding word of those who have had the management of the Erie County Agricultural Society in their care. Each succeeding Board of Managers has taken up the work where its predecessor left off and has made a sincere effort to carry on consistently with the advancement of the times. The present Board of Managers appreciates full well that this One Hundredth Anniversary Erie County Fair would not have been possible had it not been for the loyalty of the people of the county and their appreciation of the efforts which have gone into the years. More than a word is due, also, to the encouragement the management has constantly received from the Erie County Board of Supervisors. Every effort has been made to maintain the traditions of good faith and honest dealing established by the founders of this Society, and it is with this thought that the Board of Managers presents to its friends the Erie County Fair of 1940, One Hundred Years Old!

1980's

It was in 1985 that the Erie County Society took a bold step that would eventually complete the circle begun in 1942, when it accepted the Buffalo Raceway, operated by Delaware North Companies, Inc., to its grounds, and highly remunerative pari-mutuel racing opened on its track, both winter and summer.

Now 43 years later, negotiations were afoot by Society to purchase this prime tenant's holdings, a tenant whose rentals had helped improve the Fair's grounds, barns and grandstand. In addition, the Raceway had paid a substantial part of the fairgrounds' utility costs down the years, including the charge for electric power and sewerage.

It would be the next decade before the deal was closed.

Erie County Department of Environment and Planning representative Chester Janzinski reported to New York State Farm Bureau leaders on tour of Erie County in 1992, that agricultural sales exceed $100 million; inclusion of labor, fertilizer, machinery, processing and transportation would raise it to $500 million.

David E. Weaver, Cornell Cooperative Extension Agent, a leader in animal science in both Erie and Wyoming Counties, reports census figures indicate there are approximately 1,200 farms in Erie County, with a population of about 4,800, or approximately 5 percent of the 900,000 population.

Cicero Jabez Hamlin and Henry Clay Jewett of East Aurora, New York, were rival breeders of trotting and pacing horses. They established Western New York as an internationally-knows horse-breeding center.

Mr. Hamlin bred and owned The Abbot, champion trotting horse of the world.

Mr. Jewett owned the mile-long covered racetrack for winter training of trotters; it was the only completely enclosed mile-long horse track in the world, and was listed in Ripley's "Believe It or Not" in 1938. The Jewett Farm exported many light harness racers to Europe and other parts of the world.

Local Artist Thelma Winter created the Fair's 1997 poster from a photo taken by Angel Art, Ltd.

The 158th
Erie County Fair & Exposition
August 7-17, 1997

1990's

The Agricultural Vision
Chapter 16

The "Rug Ladies" Nancy Ellington and Kim Scheinder demonstrate rug hooking in the Historical Building

Historically, the 1990's could be referred to as decade of violence. Through its ten years it was witness to such horrific acts as bombings in New York City and Oklahoma City, riots in Los Angeles, warring in the Middle East and Yugoslavia, and numerous fatal shooting in America's schools, just to name a few.

For the Erie County Fair and Exposition, the '90s were a decade of change and expansion, opening with a wet Fair season that failed to put a damper on its festivities. Although there was a fifty-cent increase in admission, 1990 attendance reached 731,020. Events ranged from sheep herding demonstrations to winetastings. While the public's eye was on the Middle East, the Oak Ridge Boys and Anne Murray entertained fairgoers in 1990.

Entries in creative competitions continued to display a high level of craftsmanship and ingenuity. The winning quilt, designed by Shirley Kelly of Colden, beautifully depicted her birthplace in Nova Scotia. The quilt wowed the crowds as well as the judges.

Jean E. Muck, director of the Canned Goods Section noted that the quality and creativity of the entries was on the rise,

1990's

however the total number of entries was waning. A good example would be a jar of corn entered in the 1991 competition featuring "Erie County Fair" painstakingly spelled out in red pepper strips along the inside of the jar.

The most progressive addition to the Hamburg Fairgrounds was the completion of the International Agri-

Center. The Center is a 74,000 square, multi-purpose facility and was the concept and desire of CEO Paul Laing. Ground breaking began in the fall of '89, and was completed in 1990. The Center's intent was to house large regional agricultural events, such as horse and cattle shows. When completed, the cost of building was $4.5 million. In the off-season, the Center is booked 95% of the year with consumer and business to business trade shows and meetings. The Agri-Center, during the Fair, attracts over 200 exhibitors to sell their wares. Other attractions in 1990 a John Philip Sousa Concert by an award-winning 65-piece orchestra, guides in the barns to help "city slickers" better understand the animals and farm life, a life-size cow replica covered in 67,000 M&Ms (to help underscore the "milk" in "milk chocolate"), a 4-H Guide Dog Recognition Event, an Old-Tyme Fiddlers Contest and several new competition categories in the Horse Show.

The death of Paul Laing, the Fair's CEO and general manager, at the close of 1990 dealt an unexpected blow to everyone in the Society. Mr. Laing's contributions had helped the Fair break attendance records year after year. In testament to his outstanding achievements, Mr. Laing was posthumously inducted into the IAFE (International Association of Fairs & Expositions) Hall of Fame in 1993.

Two local women tied for the 1991 A.R. Clauss Memorial Challenge Trophy at the Horse Show. The winning horses were Odin Ridden by Tibby Hunt, and Capital Gains ridden by Linda Rosenthal. The winning riders commended the excellent course as one carefully designed to create a maximum challenge to jumpers. Throughout the '90s the Horse Show expanded with more categories. Additional horse divisions joined the Fair roster this decade, helping to maintain our status as one of the premier horse show centers in the East.

The pride, dedication and skills of 4-H youths showing their livestock continued to be a very special aspect of the Fair experience. Participants talked to Buffalo News reporters at length about the tremendous positive impact their 4-H experience had on their lives. The responsibility of caring for their animals brought these children a heightened level of maturity and discipline in all their endeavors. The 1990 Grand Champion weighed in at 1,170 pounds and earned Beth Gabel of Chaffee $2.20 lb. at auction.

Long-time
Fair traditions continued to please the crowds. The 1990 Midway offered 36 rides providing varying degrees of fun or terror. The Spirit of Youth was created in 1990, which was made up of approximately 40 talented Western New York senior students. The youth troupe consisted of a 10-piece band, singers and dancers who not only performed each day in the Outdoor Theater during the Fair, but also traveled and performed at high profile summer events to promote the Fair. The loss of 2 major sponsors caused the end of the group after the 1999 Fair. Several Spirit of Youth members went on to perform professionally on Broadway.

When could an agricultural society feel ambivalent about rain during a summer plagued by drought? Perhaps when it comes as violent thunderstorms during that society's annual fair. However, even torrential downpours couldn't dampen 1991's Erie County Fair and Exposition success. A record-breaking 788,873 attended, with totals boosted by record-breaking first-Sunday and first-Monday attendance.

Even four Tibetan monks couldn't resist the call of the Fair. The monks were enjoying a break from creating an elaborate sand mandala at the Buffalo Museum of Science—and what better way to discover the "real" America than at America's County Fair? The monks were duly impressed by the size and beauty of the animals exhibited by 4-H members.

The 1991 theme "Salute to Canada" inspired our neighbors to the north to contribute some interesting additions to the Fair (even those thunderstorms first developed over Canada). A 1,200 sq. ft. display by the Ontario Science Centre

1990's

Spirit of Youth

Lewis G. Van Ord of Russell, PA, introduced fairgoers to his 9-year-old Irish Dexter oxen, Amos and Andy. The team can pull up to 4,500 pounds.

themed, "The Seeing Brain," added a new dimension to the educational offerings. And sand sculptures of Queen Elizabeth II and Canadian Prime Minister Brian Mulroney helped keep everyone in a Canadian mood.

After the unexpected passing of the president, Paul Laing, Lloyd L. Lamb was named general manager and CEO of the Fair in 1990. New directors to the Erie County Agricultural Society were O. Fred Hofmann, a Springville potato farmer, and Joyce G. Laing, widow of the former Secretary/Manager and a retired Eden school teacher. Ms. Laing was the first woman to serve on the board in the Society's 150-year history. Joseph Solomon of West Seneca, a past Society chairman, accepted the invitation to return to that position. Sadly, Benjamin DeYoung, Jr., a long-time director, Fair Manager and past president of the Society passed away in 1991.

Highlights of the 1991 Fair included appearances by the famed Budweiser Clydesdale team, a Civil War Encampment, lumberjack competitions, moon rocks, and headliners Reba McEntire and Alabama. The A.R. Clauss Memorial Trophy and $1,000 purse went to Leigh Fischer Clark and her gelding, Nebulous.

With record-breaking attendance in 1991, what could the Fair do in 1992? Break another record! Ten days of great weather in an otherwise un-summery summer helped deliver 844,201 happy fairgoers. In fact, August 16th, 1992, brought the largest crowd ever to attend the Fair on a single day: 135,015.

With a decrease in population of 10,000 in Western New York, the fair's attendance was expected to continue breaking records. How was the Agricultural Society planning to continue consistent growth with a shrinking market. The Society's astute and thoughtful management throughout the '90s assured that the Fair was well-run, safe, clean, and accessible—no small task when you're talking about coordinating hundreds of vendors and meeting the needs of hundreds of thousands of spectators over the span of a few days.

Being well run also allowed the Fair to attract quality entertainers and vendors. Buffalo News reporters interviewed

vendors who said they returned to the Erie County Fair year after year because it was so well organized and the people were so friendly. These same vendors said there were other events across the country but they would not participate in because those two key characteristics were lacking.

The commitment of showcasing and educating the public about agriculture remained prominent on the minds of the Society and Board of Directors. As agriculture changed, so did the competitions, exhibits and displays. The number of working farms in New York State in the 1990's were 36,000 farms. Technology, economics and keener business practices made today's farmer produce more than its forefathers. The Erie County Fair, along with comparable size Fairs, worked closely with the farm industry to keep up with the innovative equipment, technology and trends. Highlighting 4-H competitions, public awareness programs and open classes will continue to be the mainstay of agricultural education for the public.

The publics' perception of the fair is that it draws a majority of attendees being from the agricultural and farm community, but in reality, the ag-community accounts for less than 5% of our attendees.

Its stellar reputation allowed the Fair to book favorite entertainment year after year. Joie Chitwood's Chevy Thunder Show marked its 50th anniversary of performing at the Erie County Fair and Expo in 1993. Crowd-pleasers such as pigs and ducks that "Dash for the Mash," pony-riding chimps — and more — could all be counted on returning to the Fair year after year.

1990's

175

But, the Society realized that established favorites must be mixed with innovative new attractions to keep the Fair vital. Along with the return of popular acts, every year in the decade brought new events and entertainment. In 1992, new additions included a cheerleading competition and 5K race—not exactly said standbys of days-gone-by.

Another very important part of a successful Fair is value. The Society worked tirelessly throughout the '90s to keep prices down and give fairgoers a grand day for their dollar. By watching every penny and partnering with local sponsors, the Society was able to offer special value opportunities and to pack the Fair full of non-stop fun at no additional charge.

Fairgoers during the '90s were treated to an amazing array of free attractions: an authentic Native American village complete with traditional dancing and craft demonstrations, daily circus performances, nationally recognized horse shows, and numerous stage shows ranging from a hypnotist to the Nelson Riddle Orchestra to popular local rock bands. At its peak, the Society invested up to $500,000 per year in entertainment offered free to those attending the Fair.

1990's

The Society also strived to have the Fair appeal to a wide variety of interests. It was a showcase that exposed '90s crowds to a little bit of everything. Where else could you have watched demonstrations of woodcarving, chair caning, logrolling, sheep shearing, blacksmithing, amazing non-stick cookware and Irish dancing all in the same day? Historical exhibits, health-screening stations and educational displays were as much a part of the Fair experience as Midway rides and parades. Variety even described the culinary delights with Greek, Italian, Mexican, and Asian delicacies offered by vendors along with Fair favorites such as saltwater taffy.

Throughout the '90s, the Society continued to remain true to its original mission of promoting agriculture. That also happened to be the crucial element that made the Fair the unique, beloved family event that it is. For, even as the number

Amanda Trinkle waits her turn as sister Alicia shares Papa's (Bob Zeigel) ice cream

of farm families dwindled, agriculture continued to be the backbone of our county economy with sales totaling $71 million each year. And that special relationship between the land, the animals and man remained an intricate part of our daily lives.

The Society made certain that everyone from grandparents to toddlers got the opportunity to enjoy watching the dedicated 4-Hers diligently tend to their animals. Everyone had the chance to experience the thrill of seeing newborn piglets struggling for prime position to suckle at their mother's teats. These are wonders that modern families can't experience anyplace else.

In the months before his passing, Mr. Laing presided over the Society's purchase of the Buffalo Raceway facilities and a subsequent $350,000 renovation. As Buffalo Raceway celebrated its 50th anniversary, the Society sought new and innovative ways to revitalize this crucial lynchpin of its holdings. Having attracted the fourth largest crowd in its history the previous year by combining a concert by the band, America, with a racing event, the Raceway added three concert events to the summer racing season in 1992.

By 1993, the Society had poured over $1 million in capital improvements into the clubhouse, track lighting and more. Fall racing was included on the schedule for the first time in 34 years and the schedule extended through three quarters of the year by the following year. However, with harness racing continuing to wane in popularity across the country, the Raceway struggled financially throughout the '90s. In 2000, the county agreed to give $175,000 in Off-Track Betting profits back to the Raceway.

In 1993, the Fair expanded from a 10-day event to an 11-day event. That helped to bring in another record-breaking year. Total attendance reached 898,907. The previous year's single-day attendance record was also broken with 141,002 fairgoers on Sunday, August 15, 1992.

Fair admission in 1993 was the same as the previous year: $6 for adults, $4 for seniors and $2.50 for children ages 6 to 12. The year saw more free entertainment including wandering clowns that interacted with children around the fairgrounds. An additional wristband day was added, brining to four the number of days attendees could enjoy unlimited rides for a fixed admission price. The motorcycle race was replaced by a motor cross event. Chuck wagon and chariot races were also added.

Highlights of national news in 1993 included the swearing-in of President Clinton, World Trade Center bombing and Federal Agent struggles with the Branch Davidian cult in Waco, Texas. The highlights of the 1993 Erie County Fair included an antique steam show of working farm equipment, a 5K race, the ever-popular World's Largest Demolition Derby, and headliners Chet Atkins (with the Buffalo Philharmonic Orchestra), John Kay & Steppenwolf, and Hank Williams, Jr. The grand champion steer of the Junior Beef Show was owned and shown by Scott Nagel of Springville.

1990's

The Fair was never meant to be merely a spectator event. From its start, it was designed to be a participatory experience. That held true over 150 years later. Even in the '90s, the Fair thrived on community involvement. Community members were invited to showcase their skills by entering the many competitions in wide-ranging categories. You could find a competitions ranging from cheerleading to agricultural engineering.

Competitions for historical displays exposed fairgoers to everything from the making of old-time bathtub gin to the evolution of lacrosse. Art and photography sections provided a forum for creative individuals of all ages and backgrounds to display their work. Even unusual arts could find a place at the Fair — Robert Baldo of Hamburg took home a Tricolor ribbon for his model of a Mississippi riverboat, a project that involved 4,379 pieces of wood and three years of construction.

Homemakers were invited to enter their quilts, canned goods, sewing projects and more. You didn't have to be a farm girl to bake a blue-ribbon-winning pie. In fact, you didn't even have to be a girl. During the '90s, entries submitted by boys and men were starting to show up in many of the categories previously dominated by females. Also during the '90s, entries were solicited from outside Erie County. Individuals from throughout Western New York were invited to participate in Fair competitions.

Mary Jane Smith proudly displays award winning doilie

Not only did you not have to be a farmer to have prize-winning produce this decade, non-farmers actually had a distinct advantage over working farmers. Hobby horticulturalists who had more time and resources to lovingly tend a few vegetables in their backyards could reap better-looking harvests than the farmer who tended acres of crops. And age was no barrier to winning some of the competitions. In fact, the 1994 Tricolor award in the flower show went to 7-year-old Lindsay Guzzetta of North Boston for her marigolds. Most of the competitions at the Fair let the winner take home cash as well as a ribbon. Purses varied from a few dollars to several hundred depending on the event. A winning pie in the Pillsbury Refrigerated Piecrust Championship (introduced in 1998) might take home $125 (and the winner didn't even have to make the crust from scratch)! The Horse Show prize money totaled upwards of $30,000 each year. And of course, the swine, beef and lamb auction tended to be especially rewarding for prizewinners. In 1996 alone 4-H youngsters brought home over $100,000 from the auction.

Organizations as well as individuals were are also encouraged to participate in the Fair. The 1990s saw numerous groups using the Fair as their forum: lawyers providing answers to consumers' legal questions, charities distributing information on their causes, schools showcasing the talents of their students, and more.

As much as the community was an integral part of the Fair, the Society strove to be an active, positive force in the community. Thousands of free Fair tickets were distributed each year to group homes, scouting organizations, charities and others so that the underprivileged, disabled and deserving could attend the Fair. The Society saw to it that every Fair featured health screenings, consumer safety demonstrations, distribution of senior citizen ID cards, environmental educational exhibits and other events that could help people improve life in Erie County and beyond.

1990's

Plus, profits continued to be poured back into the fairgrounds to maintain the quality of the Fair experience for all. The Fair strove to be a good neighbor. The Society scrupulously attended to safety, cleanliness and quality. And fairgoers poured thousands of dollars into local businesses ranging from gas stations to restaurants.

In 1994 the Fair's innovative plant beds earned a Silver Tray Beautification Award from the Professional Plant Growers Association. The Society invited area growers to recommend the plants to be showcased in the Fair's 14 beds. These trial beds provided an ideal way for growers to show off new introductions and for the public to see how the new flowers perform. Leave it to the efficient-minded members of the Society to even put the landscaping to better use!

Other highlights of 1994 included an attempt at the world's largest country line dance, a high-tech Adventure Zone, and a special exhibit of llamas near the Livestock Arena. Attendance records were broken yet again with 900,029 fairgoers at the 11-day event. The single-day attendance record was broken with 147,312 fairgoers on Sunday.

In 1994 Eugene W. Hock was named chairman of the Society board. George G. Sipprell, longtime Society treasurer passed away. Headliners for 1994 included Tanya Tucker, Weird Al Yankovic and Vince Gill.

In 1995 the Fair exhibits included more animals than ever, almost 15,000. A whopping 9,700 of those were 4-H entries, the largest number of 4-H entries ever. For the first time in Fair history, camels and sharks were included in the offerings. Four 8' sharks were displayed in a 9,000-gallon tank. Also new, the Wild Ones Show featured trick skateboard, BMX bike and in-line skate exhibitions.

Throughout the '90s, motor events remained strong attractions. The tractor pulls involving gargantuan machines straining to move even larger loads, and the freewheeling crash-and-burn spectacles of the demolition derbies were hugely popular grandstand events.

1990's

Attendance in '95 broke yet another record, topping 1 million. Revenues were up substantially with an $833,784 post-Fair surplus. This was quite an amazing accomplishment when you consider it in context. As the area prepared to celebrate the upcoming Centennial of Buffalo's Pan-Am Exhibition it became evident how grand that exhibition had been, how prominent a city Buffalo had been. While the city was significant in size and stature, 100 years later its populations and fortunes had dwindled. Yet, the Fair had grown to amazing proportions even as local populations shrunk. And the Fair had not always occupied its present home. Before 1868, the Fair was held at a variety of locations including the Cold Spring section of Buffalo and the corner of Elk and Dygert in Springville.

In 1995 Richard L. Campbell, a Newstead attorney, was named chairman of the Society. He stated that his goal was to "keep up the fair's tradition, always trying to improve and make it better." The Agri-Center was on schedule with its loan repayment and increasing in bookings each year.

Also in 1995, the Hamburg Grange No. 1293 named Margaret Lockwood "Citizen of the Year". Having attended 90 Erie Country Fairs, many of them as a worker, Mrs. Lockwood served as director emeritus of the Creative Arts Board of which she was a past president. Mrs. Lockwood and her son Harry also began serving on the Society's Board of Directors. Known to many as "My Fair Lady," Ms. Lockwood personified the spirit of dedication of the many individuals who helped make the Fair a quality event each year. Mrs. Lockwood passed away in 1998.

Margaret Lockwood with son Harry at her last Fair in 1997

1990's

Another 'Fair' lady was Kelly Falgiene, who won the 1995 Miss Erie County Fair Pageant, and also later represented the State the New York in the Miss America Pageant.

In 1996 a winning lottery ticket was sold at the Fair. Thomas and Linda Callaghan of Appleton were $17 million dollars richer from their experience at the Fair. New free events in '96 included the Artie Shaw Orchestra, Beatlemania, Wheel of Fortune Live with Bob Eubanks, comedians Williams and Ree, Hawthorn white tigers, Incredible Nooks aerial daredevil team, and the Alexander 8-Horse Mini Hitch horse team.

Frank Newton, the Society's most senior director and an individual who had pioneered the causes of conservation and environmentalism was honored as a Citizen of the Week. Lillian Cheeseman who faithfully served the Buffalo Raceway from 1942 to 1967 passed away.

The '96 attendance topped 1 million but failed to beat the '95 record. Promotion via a Fair website brought visitors from far and wide. One gentlemen from Germany said he decided to stop at the Fair after discovering the website. Prior to the event, the site was receiving 4,000 to 10,000 hits a day.

While not part of the Fair itself, WNY's largest indoor craft show was held on the Hamburg Fairgrounds each winter. It was ranked number one in the nation in 2000 (up from #5 in 1997) by Sunshine Artist magazine. The hugely popular "Christmas in the Country" craft show was just one of the shows making the Agri-Center its home during the off-season. Other shows featured cooking, woodworking, home improvement, guns, antiques and more.

The Agri-Center was blessed with a variety of advantages that made it attractive to events organizers. Its location close to a NY State Thruway exit made it highly accessible. Being on the fairgrounds, the community awareness of the location was high. Parking was plentiful and the center itself was a spacious, flexible venue.

The Erie County 4-H program had significant increases in participation for the Fair in 1997. Although Dairy entries were down, beef entries' figures doubled those of 1998. Swine entries brought an all time high average of $2.29 a pound. The 4-H also opened a "Snack'n Healthy" snack bar near the barns and show ring. Getting fresh produce from local farms, the snack bar got rave reviews.

Although severe storms kept the attendance figures for 1997 just shy of one million, the entertainment arranged by Entertainment Coordinator Ron Erickson and Fair Manager Lloyd Lamb reached a diverse audience. Motor event lovers were treated to the ARDC Championship Midget Auto Racing, Chitwood Chevy Thunder Show, annual NTPA Truck and Tractor Pull, and three Demolition Derbies. Every local television network and local papers also reported Robbie Knievel's jump over 16 CID garbage trucks, which broke his father, Evil Knievel's, record. Music lovers enjoyed The Rock N' Roll Rebel Tour featuring John Kay and

Steppenwolf, and Grandstand acts like Hank Williams Jr., Travis Tritt, Charlie Daniels, and Jo Dee Messina.

In 1998, the Fair, with its theme, "Out of this World," saw WNY native and NASA astronaut, Lt. William Gregory come to the Fair and discuss his experiences in space. Headliners in 1998 included Tracy Lawrence, Clint Black, Pam Tillis, Savage Garden, Chuck Negron, and Gallagher.

1998 also saw the largest attendance for the 11-day event, coming in at 1,020,662. Admission prices for 1998 were set at $7 for adults, and $3 for children ages 6 to 12. David Schlabach of East Aurora was appointed manager of the Fair in '98. Lloyd Lamb continued to fill the position of CEO. That same year, Dr. Kevin O'Gorman of Eden was appointed a director on the Society's board.

In 1999, the Fair added a Baboon Lagoon wild animal show, a 170-foot-long Giant Slide, an inexpensive helicopter ride, and a Rock Carver who created fountains out of a slab of rock, while the crowd looked on.

Since education and education are very important facets to the Fair, a new "Agricultural Guide to the Fair" was introduced. Educational information included pigs, llamas, cows, horses, profile of three local farm families, dictionary and Western New York Agricultural Fun Facts. "Ag Tag," where 15 questions were asked and the answers could be found on signs throughout the fairgrounds, was also started. Receiving over 400 entries, the Fair achieved its purpose of educating the layman and bringing the agricultural community together with the general public.

"Miles of Smiles," the theme to the 1999 Fair, attracted an attendance of 1,001,927.

Late in 1999, Dennis R. Lang of West Seneca was appointed general manager and CEO of the Fair. His goal for the Fair was to "have a little different twist." He felt that people "want to be entertained, but even more, they want to be educated and entertained at the same time."

Across the country, several county fairs have reluctantly had to merge with other fairs due to the rise of insurance, cost of bills and talent, therefore, to succeed in today's society, it was decided that the Erie County Fair must be managed as a business.

1990's

For the 2000 Fair, Lang's goal to make the Fair more affordable and interactive prompted a daring promotion: the price of admission for the first day of the Fair was just 25 cents! A 1900s theme accompanied the promotion with staff members in period costumes, old-fashioned events, and vendors encouraged to offer items at 1900 prices, a promotion that increased attendance over 400%.

The promotion was a big hit with the public. Unfortunately, Mother Nature did not seem to approve. The previous night, severe thunderstorms turned portions of the Fair parking lots to mush. The ever-resourceful Society soon had alternate parking in place, with fairgoers directed to Ralph Wilson Stadium parking lots where buses shuttled them to the fairgrounds. However, the combination of the parking problem and the huge crowds swarming in for the promotion caused traffic delays of up to hours.

Also in 2000, the agricultural area was the focus of more inter-activity and increased displays. The Ag-Sperience included a Mooternity Ward, an Ag Tag game and fun activities for the kids. For the first time ever, the Fair was host to the Empire State Junior Preview Classic, a show featuring Grand Champion Cattle from throughout the US and Canada. Therapeutic Riding was introduced and fireworks were brought back after a 10-year absence. Headliners included Jethro Tull, Trisha Yearwood and Lonestar. Attendance in 2000 was 1,006,350.

In 2000, a fire aboard one of the Strates Show train cars left 11 Strates employees homeless, but no one was seriously injured. The Strates Shows that visited the Fair each year were the only remaining midway shows in America which continued to travel by train from town to town.

As 2000 marked the 50th anniversary of the Korean War, a monument dedicated to the veterans of that war was unveiled during a special ceremony at the fairgrounds. Memorial services, a parade of military organizations and plantings dedicated to the veterans were all part of the Society's solemn salute of those who gave their lives for their country.

1990's

185

Since its beginning in 1821, the Erie County Agricultural Society has stuck to its agricultural foundation. This vision continues to be the core of the Fair's existence. It is this unique advantage that draws crowds from miles away and separates the Fair from a common carnival. Everyone has the opportunity to get up close and personal with rural life, meeting the animals and the people who tend them and getting a taste for the past, present and future of farm activities.

Throughout the '90s, it was Society's continued focus on agriculture that allowed the Erie Country Fair and Exposition to maintain its position as America's County Fair. And, as stated by CEO/Fair Manager Dennis Lang prior to the 2000 Fair, it is this focus that will keep the Erie County Fair and Exposition enduring throughout the new millenium.

"Entering into the new millenium presents many new opportunities for all of us. ...We are ever striving to enhance the agricultural and historical legacy of our great Fair as we educate Western New Yorkers of the impact agriculture has on all our lives. As farming techniques improve, we too will be paving the way for an evolution of sorts, keeping pace with the needs of Americans whose ancestors built the foundation of our great country. If we make mistakes along the way, we will learn from them and strive to become bigger and better."

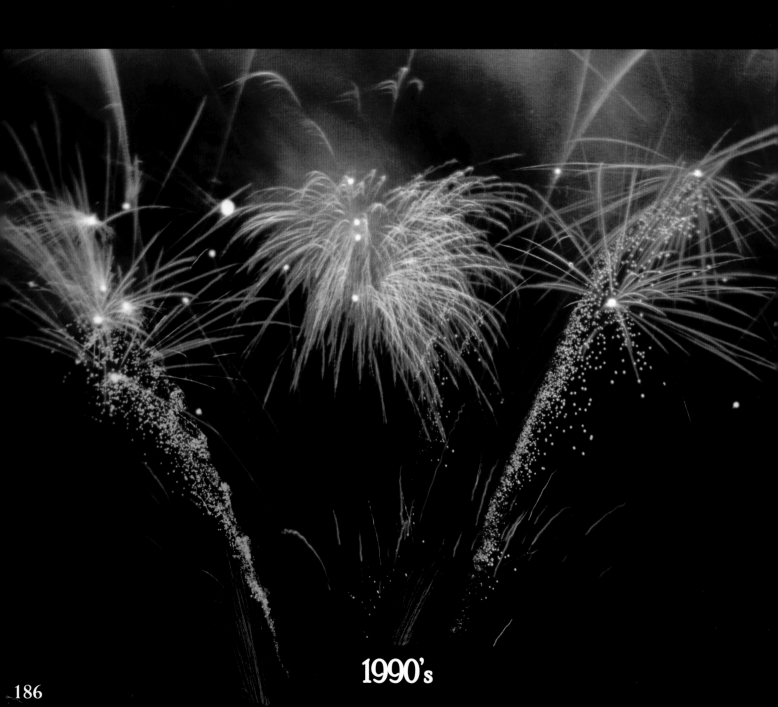

1990's

Ron Erickson
with Jethro Tull

The Past and the Present...

*This insert won 1st place in the 2001
Buffalo News Creative Arts Advertising Award
Competition.*

*The winning page was created by
Lou Ann Delaney and Holly Smyczynski*

EXTRA

BUFFALO EVENING NEWS

ERIE COUNTY FAIR EDITION

VOL. I - NO. I | BUFFALO, N.Y., THURSDAY, AUGUST 10, 2000 | FREE

OPENING DAY SPECIAL NEWSPAPER

25¢ ADMISSION FOR EVERYONE

No Need to Break the Bank at Opening Day of the Erie County Fair.

We Are Rolling Back Our Prices to the General Admission Charged at the Beginning of the 20th Century.

SUMMERING AT THE ERIE COUNTY FAIR

ECAS, sponsors of the Erie County Fair, salutes the 1900s and prepares for the new millennium.

When we think of county fairs, we think of mom and apple pie, Americana, red, white and blue. Actually, the history of fairs can be traced to the dawn of agriculture (approximately 6000 B.C.). Harvest time was the perfect time to meet, exhibit and trade both agricultural products and handmade wares.

The first fairs in the American colonies were market fairs in the European tradition. On Manhattan Island in 1625 a fair for the sale of cattle and hogs was held. Soon after in 1641 the first-ever cattle fair in a bit of territory called Cow Neck (now the Manhasset-Port Washington area) was held.

The father of the American Agricultural Fair was a gentleman farmer from Pittsfield, Mass., named Elkanah Watson. Watson served General Washington in the Revolution and in 1779 he became the liaison for Benjamin Franklin in Paris. During his years in Europe, Watson traveled extensively and kept an eye out for the improvement of American agriculture and commerce.

At the age of 50, Elkanah Watson bought a farm in Pittsfield with a strong desire to help develop America's agricultural resources. In 1807 he acquired a pair of Merino sheep imported from Spain. Watson took the pure white pair to the village green to exhibit them to his neighbors.

One year later the Pittsfield farmer pointed out that the long-legged, large-boned hogs the locals were breeding were unprofitable. He introduced his Massachusetts neighbors to a strain of short-legged swine from Dutchess County, N.Y. Watson also showed local farmers how to improve the cattle population with a superior type of English breeding bull and how to dig private ponds, stocking them with fresh-water table fish.

OPENING DAY 100 YEARS AGO —

FROM A VANTAGE POINT ABOVE THE MIDWAY, LOOKING DOWN THE AVENUE OF FLAGS

The growing interest in Watson's discoveries encouraged him to plan a much larger event. So in October of 1810 the first American Agricultural Fair was born. It featured a music band, a parade, a float display, an operating broadcloth loom and a working spinning jenny, and pens filled with a variety of prize-quality animals. One feature of the procession was a plow, drawn by 69 chained oxen, driven by the oldest man in the county. Marchers wore badges of wheat in their hats as a reminder of the main theme: agriculture.

The following year the Berkshire Agricultural Society formed and the second county fair was held. Over 3,000 people attended the 1811 fair which offered prizes totaling $70 awarded to the best livestock. Women participated for the first time in 1813, competing in cooking, needlework and other household-arts products.

The county agricultural fair was in the farmer's own best interest, and he knew it. It was a means of education and incentive toward a better life. It also took care of the farm family's social-entertainment needs for a few days out of the working year — that, too, is beneficial. Innovation in farming equipment was demonstrated in the 1830s, with new farm machines like the Cyrus McCormick's reaper and John Deere's steel plow, developed in 1837. What better way to exhibit the new machines to farmers who could examine the latest agricultural aids?

As state governments became larger and more prosperous they took an interest in agriculture. In 1941, the nation's first state fair was held at the village of Syracuse in New York state. Today state fairs are held in nearly every state in the nation. Nationwide there are over 3,200 fairs from each region of America.

The American revolutionary spirit of "Lets show 'em boys" created a unique institution out of the old European style market fair that lives today in state and county agricultural fairs across the nation.

The Erie County Agricultural Society was formed in 1819 and held the first Erie County Fair in 1820 on the current site of the Donovan Office Building in Buffalo. The fair moved to Hamburg in 1868.

Today, agriculture remains New York's number one industry and has survived the trials of growth and technology. The Erie County Fair will continue to honor its heritage and will keep its eyes open for tomorrow. It is our goal to impact and educate our community, to instill pride and appreciation for the work involved and the people behind the food that we eat.

The next time we sit down for a meal, thank God and thank a farmer.

STUNT SHOW IS A LONGSTANDING TRADITION

Not as Reckless as They Used to Be

In the 1940s, the Erie County Fair held auto stunt shows with drivers Kochmann and Chitwood that included two- and four-car precision driving, reverse spins, with crash stunts that included the Human Battering Ram, T-bone crashes and roll-overs. We invite you to come out and set your eyes on some of the old and new tricks in the Millennium edition of the Toyota Hollywood Auto Stunt Show on Tuesday, Aug. 15.

HATS OFF TO THEIR SERVICE

These concessionaires have been at the Fair for several years. We thank them for their continued support.

Congratulations on your 50th year at our Fair
Jimmy Smith — Independent Games

40+ years
Burt Weidner Chicken BBQ — at the Erie County Fair for 45 years
Fowlers Taffy and Kitchen Maid Candy for 40 years each

30+ years
Pinelli Foods — 37 years ago started delivering meat on the grounds for Strates Shows
Tootsie's Fried Dough — thank you Rene Piche!

Be Sure to Stop By These Stands and Say Hi

Dennis R. Lang
CEO, Erie County Fair Manager

WELCOME TO OPENING DAY AT ERIE COUNTY FAIR 2000

Thank you for joining us for a special day that we've designed in honor of the last century. It's a good time to reflect on and to honor an industry that we must understand and support: agriculture.

The 21st century will bring as many changes as this past century. If we ignore and fail to learn from our history, the next century and our children's future could be in jeopardy. Today, we invite our neighbors and community to celebrate the past, the world of agriculture and the impact it has had on our lives. The Erie County Fair celebrates its 161st anniversary and as we've reviewed the last century, we would like to salute the 1900s: its mistakes, its inventions and, most importantly, the good times we and our forefathers have experienced. Leave the computers off today and enjoy; be thankful for where we are today and why.

As the 19th century drew to a close, the Commercial Advertiser gave the Society (known now as the Erie County Agricultural Society) a fine send off into the 20th, which would so revolutionize American farm life, quoted as saying: "The Association pays premiums which would amount to thousands of dollars, but sometimes they run very close to the cushion. This year, as the 41st Annual Erie County Fair, there will be plenty of money for all expenses and probably a good balance to apply to the debt of the Society, incurred by the purchase of additional grounds about four years ago. The officers are delighted with the outlook."

We are proud to kick off, 100 years later, the 161st edition of the Erie County Fair in the 21st Century. One hundred years ago there were 226,720 farms in New York state and currently there are 38,000 (8,200 of which are dairy farms). You do the math. Though the numbers may seem ominous, through science, teamwork and determination, these same farms exceed the production of farms from the early 1900s and help to feed the world.

Today, agriculture remains at the top of Western New York's leading industries list. Learn about agriculture and continue to support and thank our farmers for their determination and hard work. Keep our legacy alive!

– Denny

FARE DEALS

STOP BY THESE VENDORS FOR SPECTACULAR SAVINGS

Santillo Sausage Inc.
42nd Street
Italian Sausage $3.00, Cheesesteak $3.25, Cheeseburger $1.50, Hamburger $1.25, Hot dogs $1.00, Cold Drinks 16 oz., $1.00 24 oz. $1.50

Rainbow Rentals
Midway & Gate 4
Strollers $5.00
Wagons $10.00
Wheel Chairs $10.00

Potato House
Behind Grandstand
Old Fashioned Cone Cup Filled with French Fries 25¢

Bert Weidner Farms Chicken BBQ
Behind Grandstand
$1.00 off Chicken BBQ Dinner

Weidner's Steak
Dome
Free Beverage with Purchase of T-Bone Steak Dinner

Pop Pop's Skillet
Games Road & Behind Grandstand
Fries 25¢, Wooden Nickels 50% off during Fair

Kari's Big Slice
Triangle, Fare Alley, Grandstand Drive
$2.00 off Sausage, $2.00 off Steak, $1.00 off Pizza

Diablo's Concessions
Avenue of Flags
All Tacos, Burritos & Nachos with Cheese Discounted 100 Pennies for 100 Years.

Concession Concepts Unlimited (Oxie's)
Fare Alley
$1.00 off all Dinners

Gonzalez Soulvaki
Grandstand
Buy 1 Sandwich get 1 Free Pop

Hanson's Original Kettle Korn
Historical Lane
Brown Paper bag of Kettle Korn 25¢

James Staub
Mozzarella Sticks, Chicken Fingers, Jalepeno Poppers, French Fries, Sweet Potato Fries, 50¢ off
Sno Kones 25¢, 7-oz. soft drinks 25¢

Main Street Butcher Block
Avenue of Flags
Hot Dog & Pepsi 99¢, Ice Cream Cone 99¢

Horigan's Coffee Co.
Marketplace Patio
50¢ off all Drinks, Regular Coffee any size $1.00

Oasis Tent
Gate 4, Top Avenue of Flags
$1.00 Wristband for Entire Day

The Thomas Hodson Co.
Grandstand, Xtreme Zone
Fruit Smoothies 25¢

Buffalo Pizza Concessions
Louie's Pizza-Bazaar
$1.25 slices of Cheese & Pepperoni Pizza, Small pop 75¢

Maria's Catering
Grandstand
$2.00 off regular Dinner Platters

Pasta Express
42nd Street — Behind Grandstand
Buy 1/2 Boat of French Fries, Beverage (12-oz.) only 25¢, All Entrees $1.00 off

JMB Concessions
Bazaar Building
$1.00 off Smoothies

JPH Enterprises Inc.
Fare Alley
15% off Future Purchases of $10.00 or More, Hamburger and Hot dogs $1.00, Coffee 25¢, Sausage 2 for 1, Old-Fashioned Ice Cream Sodas 50¢, 7-oz. Beverage 25¢

Greater Buffalo Concessions
38 Park Lane
Funnel Cakes and Small Drink $1.00

Amusements of Buffalo
$1.00 off everything

Old Style Foods
Fare Alley
Roast Corn $1.00

Fat Bob's Smokehouse
Beer Gardens Entrance
Texas Turkey Legs & Beans 1/2 price

Periwinkle Enterprises
Grandstand Triangle
$1.00 off Wings

B. Wilson Enterprises
Avenue of Flags, Fare Alley
Free Ice Cream Toppings
Buy One Slice ($2.50) get One 1/2 off

Cowboy Cal's Bar-B-Que
42nd Street
Free Drink with Sandwich Purchase

Hot Dog Express
Draw Gate
Hot Dogs,Hamburgers and Pop $1.00 each

Piccolo's Food Concessions
Fare Alley
Mini Donuts 12 for $1.00

DeCapio Family Concessions
50¢ Sno Kones

D&F Enterprises
Slade Park
Soft Pretzels $1.00, Nachos & Cheese $1.00, 20 oz. Pop $1.00

TD Concessions
Grandstand Drive
Buy any Chicken Finger, Sub, Pizza Log, or BBQ Pork Chop and receive a free 12-oz. Pepsi

Louie's Texas Red Hots
42nd Street
Hot Dogs 5 for $5.00

Mantione Enterprises
Fare Alley Triangles and Historical Lane
25¢ Chocolate Chip Cookies, 50¢ off Curly Q's

Russ Pig & Ox
Fare Alley & Bazaar
$2.00 off Dinner Plate, $1.00 off Sandwiches (Pork or Beef)

Russ' Curly Fries
Fare Alley
$1.00 off Small or Large Curly Q

Kolassa Enterprises, LLC
Agri-Center, Dome, Games Road, Top of Midway
1/2 off Salt Water Taffy and Lemonade
Lime Orange Drinks, 25¢ Pepsi

Gyro & Soulvaki
Historical Lane
$1.00 off a Gyro Sandwich

Debbie's Concessions
Grandstand
$1.50 Walk-Away Sundaes

Jack's Delicious Fries
Fare Alley
75¢ off Fries, 50¢ Pepsi

F&W Concessions Inc.
Fare Alley
Free Drink with Steak, Chicken Sandwich, or Salad Purchase

Mike's Concessions
Fare Alley
25¢ Small Soda With Any Purchase

Held's
Independent Lane — Game Row 18
75¢ Hot Dogs, $1.00 Hamburgers, $1.25 Cheeseburgers

Lackawanna Masonic Lodge
Fare Alley
25¢ Coffee, $3.00 Curly Q's

Russell's Concessions
Fare Alley
Buy Either a Hard Taco or Sausage Sandwich and get a 25¢ Old-Fashioned Lemonade

Salvatore's Pizza
Triangle
75¢ Pizza Slices and Drinks

Chiavetta's Catering
Fare Alley
$3.99 BBQ Chicken Dinners

Alessi Concessionaires
Buy an Onion and get a Free Drink, 50¢ off Lemonade

Mark's Pizza & Subs
Games Road
25¢ Cheese & Nachos

Aunt Sue's Fries
Fare Alley
$1.00 off Ribbon Fries

Utter Delights
$1.00 off Milkshakes

Louie's Pizza
42nd Street, Behind Bazaar Building
$1.00 off Pizza & Pasta Dishes

Specials good only on Aug. 10, 2000.

OLDEST BUILDING ON GROUNDS

Rare Octagon Shape is Noteworthy

This octagon-shaped building is the oldest building standing on the Hamburg Fairgrounds. Originally constructed in 1885 as the Women's Department Building, the building has only been at its present location on the Avenue of the Flags since the 1940s. It was moved from its original location at the top of the Midway, taking two days to move on blocks and wheels. This 65-foot diameter building became known as the Health Building in the late '40s when a new building was constructed to house the Women's Building, which is today known as the Junior/4-H/Public Service Building. This is one of the few remaining octagon-shaped buildings in the world.

HISTORICAL BUILDING HAS STORIED CAREER

Now Itself a Historic Artifact

The Historical Building dates back to 1885, when the structure that currently serves as the building's front section was constructed as an agricultural building. This building received its name at an official dedication in 1965 by Lynda "Bird" Johnson, daughter of former president Lyndon B. Johnson. Through the efforts of Julia Boyer-Reinstein and George Sipprell, a 40 x 100' addition was built in 1971. This addition tripled the size of the original structure and now provides sufficient space to house competitive exhibits by 19 Erie County Historical Societies.

SPONSORS

The Buffalo News, Lancaster Opera House, West Herr Automotive Group, Hamburg Color Lab, Niagara Mohawk, WIVB-TV, WXRL, WHTT, Strates Shows

Special thanks to all those who helped put this day together.

Staff helping out to produce this special section …

Lou Ann Delaney • Holly Smyczynski • Jessica Gominiak

At The Buffalo News: Mark Stack

A Native American by the name of Twylah Hurd Nitch was helping a local Boy Scout Troop set up their exhibit, she noticed the original inhabitants of this area were not exhibiting their tradition. She mentioned this to County Executive, Mr. Edward Rath. She asked how she would go about setting up a Native American exhibit. He asked, "What type of village?" She answered, "a life size Indian Village." He suggested that she prepare some plans and suggestions as to where to put it and the types of activities she had in mind. Mr. Rath set a meeting up with Mr. Clayton Taylor and it was presented to the Board of Directors.

The proposal was accepted by the Board and was placed near a pond on the fairgrounds. The pond has since been filled in, but the village remained. The village was called the Nyah-weh village.

Mr. Taylor and Twylah Hurd Nitch became good friends.

The project was an answer to a dream to share their tradition with strangers of their race.

It's been told that when Mr. Taylor passed in spirit, the Village formed a circle and placed his image in the center and released his spirit in to the Lights of Peace.

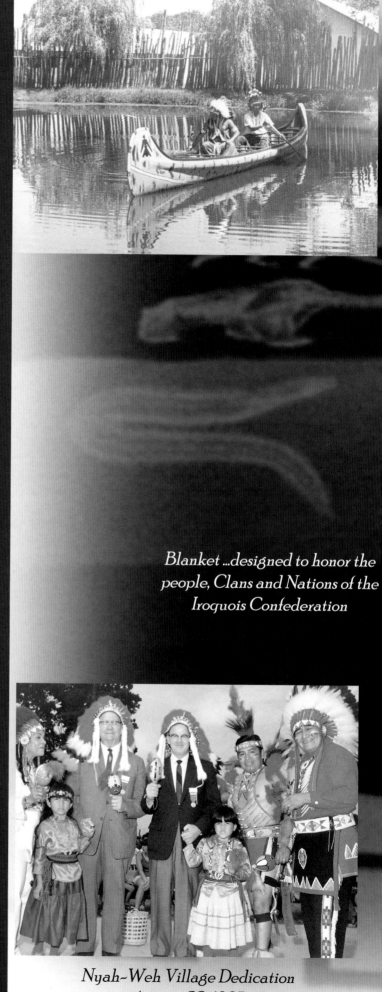

Blanket ...designed to honor the people, Clans and Nations of the Iroquois Confederation

Nyah-Weh Village Dedication
August 22, 1965

David Gorden, Mrs. Ray Hurd, Edwin Gorden

Tiny Tots Dance

"When words are spoken from the mouth and mind, not even children will listen. When words are spoken from the heart, everyone will listen."

~A Tonawanda Seneca

Erie County Agricultural Society

1933 Directors, Standing Left to Right:
E.H. Williams, William H. Abbott, Clark Hurd, Clayton Taylor, Ralph Thorn,

Seated Left to Right:
Gustave C. Miller, Fredrick Hauck, John O'Leary, Lewis E. Willet (President),

Photo courtesy of Sue Willet

Clayton Taylor
Director
1900-01

Board of Directors from the early 1900's

John Lapp, J.C. Newton (Secretary), F.H. Briggs, G.B. Abbott

Charles Brown, Frank Dorn, Charles H. Fosdick

J.P. Drummer Jr.
Director
1906

Erie County Agricultural Society Board of Directors 2000-2001

Dennis R. Lang

Ronald Geitter

O. Frederick Hofmann

Joseph M. Solomon

Lloyd L. Lamb

Robert W. Dygert, D.V.M.

Harry J. Lockwood

Kay L. Leitzan

Wesley C. Dust

Joyce C. Laing

Frank E. Newton

Earl W. Henry

Eugene. W Hock

Richard L. Campbell

Kenneth Wilk

Kevin N. O'Gorman, M.D.

DIRECTOR EMERITUS

Richard E. Cooke

Ray E. Draudt

George R. Hebard Jr.

J. William Lexo

ERIE COUNTY AGRICULTURAL SOCIETY

Presidents

1841-1842	Lewis F. Allen	Buffalo
1843-1844	Hon. Thomas E. Love	Buffalo
1845-1846	Robert McPherson	Black Rock
1847	Orlando Allen	Buffalo
1848-1849	Augustus Raynor	Buffalo
1850	Robert Persons	East Aurora
1851-1852	Apollos Hitchcock	Cheektowaga
1853	Amos Chilcott	East Hamburg
1854	John W. Hamlin	Aurora
1855	Allen Potter	East Hamburg
1856	George W. Tifft	Buffalo
1857	Erastus Wallis	East Aurora
1858-1860	Wm. Hambleton	East Hamburg
1861-1863	Z. Bonney	Buffalo
1864-1865	Geo. A. Moore	Buffalo
1866	Edwin Wright	Springville
1867	L. C. P. Vaughn	Springville
1868-1873	P. W. Powers	East Hamburg
1874-1878	V. R. Cary	Boston
1879-1880	Isaac Russell	North Collins
1881-1882	George M. Pierce	Hamburg
1883-1884	John Kraus	Clarence
1885-1887	Hiram P. Hopkins	Buffalo
1888-1892 H.	Wayne White	Hamburg
1893 -1895	Horace Landon	Eden
1896-1897	J. W. Carter	Eden Valley
1898-1899	Edward Hepp	Hamburg
1900-1901	C. C. Taylor	Lawtons
1902	Gayer Garndner	East Hamburg
1903-1905	John A. Kloepfer	Hamburg
1906-1907	Samuel W. Stuart	Hamburg
1908-1909	John A. Kloepfer	Hamburg
1910	Jacob C. Newton	East Hamburg
1911-1913	Wm. H. Abbott	Hamburg
1914	Walter C. Clark	Eden
1915-1917	R. W. Hengerer	Hamburg
1918-1920	Colon J. Dudley	Hamburg
1921-1935	Lewis E. Willet	Lackawanna
1936-1937	Charles H. Brown	Orchard Park
1938-1939	George B. Abbott	Hamburg
1940-1941	Clark W. Hurd	Elma
1942	Nelson W. Cheney	Eden
1943	Nelson W. Cheney	Eden (died - No Fair)
1943	John W. Kleis	Hamburg (replacement)

1944-1946	John W. Kleis	Hamburg
1947-1948	John K. Lapp	Clarence
1949-1950	Lyle J. Tillou	East Aurora
1951-1952	Clayton C. Taylor	Lawtons
1953-1954	Eugene P. Forrestel	Akron
1955-1956	Arthur G. Fries	Kenmore
1957	Harrison V. Baker	Hamburg (died Nov.)
1957	Fred Hauck	Hamburg (replaced Dec.)
1958-1959	Earl L. Lexo	Elma
1960-1961	Charles A. Welch	Orchard Park
1962-1963	Walter D. Henry	Eden
1964-1965	Henry H. Sylvester	Lackawanna
1966-1967	W. Howard Vanderhoef	Hamburg
1968-1969	Benjamin DeYoung, Jr.	Akron
1970-1971	John K. Thompson	Evans
1972-1973	Richard T. Cooke	Alden
1974-1975	Frank E. Newton	Orchard Park
1976-1977	George R. Hebard, Jr.	Hamburg
1978-1979	J. William Lexo	Elma
1980-1981	Earl W. Henry	Eden
1982-1983	Philip E. Richardson	Akron
1984-1985	Paul A. Lang	West Seneca
1986-1987	Ray E. Draudt	Hamburg
1988-1989	Joseph M. Solomon	West Seneca
1990	Lloyd L. Lamb	Springville
1991	Joseph M. Solomon	West Seneca
1992-1993	Dr. Robert Dyggert D.V.M	Hamburg
1994	Eugene Hock	Hamburg
1995-97	Richard Campbell	Akron
1998-1999	Dennis Lang	West Seneca
2000-2001	Ronald Geitter	Orchard Park

Women's Department Past Presidents

Mrs William Newton
President 1882

Mrs. Edgar Cheney
President 1885

Mrs. Seth A. Abbott
President 1883

Mrs. Anna Brooks
President 1929-31

Dossier of Ellen Taussig

Ellen Taussig is a Philadelphian. She attended Springside School for Girls in Chestnut Hill, Pennsylvania and the American Academy of Dramatic Art, New York.

In 1938, she began her journalistic career as a society columnist for The Philadelphia Evening Public Ledger, and then as a general news reporter and feature writer.

She continued on to The Philadelphia Daily News, The Philadelphia Record, the Camden, N.J. Post Express and the Philadelphia Evening Bulletin.

In 1949, she went to The Buffalo Evening News, now The Buffalo News, where she was on the staff for 25 years.

Upon her retirement in 1974, she wrote three books: Your Host, Peter Gust of the Park Lane Restaurant; Wings on My Heels—A Newspaper Woman's Story, and The Realization of a Doctor's Dream—The Story of the Medical Foundation of Buffalo, Inc.—During Its First Thirty Years—1956-1986.

In 1989, at the suggestion of Elizabeth Willett, head of the Reference Department of The Buffalo & Erie County Public Library, Paul C. Laing, secretary of the Erie County Agricultural Society and general manager of its Erie County Fair & Expo, commissioned her to write the 150-year history of the Society (1841-1989).

Ellen Taussig has had an unusually wide and varied journalistic career, in Philadelphia, Western New York and Ontario, Canada.

In 1974, The Niagara Frontier Folk Art Council, Inc. commended her for "journalistic promotion of the ethnic heritage of the Niagara Frontier."

The Newspaper Guild, AFL-FIO, twice cited her for journalistic performance.

Her series on leading families of Buffalo will be recalled by readers, and her descriptions of historic houses throughout Western New York will be familiar, as will her coverage of visits of the Royal Family to Canada, and interviews with the wives of four presidents of the United States.

Ellen Taussig writes a column in the Cape May Star and Wave newspaper, called "Memory Lane," for senior citizens, telling of their experiences, opinions and accomplishments in Cape May, N.J. where she now lives.

With Thanks from Ellen

My sincere thanks go to Erna Eaton of the Editorial Staff of the Buffalo News, who edited this book; to Miss Ruth J. Willett, head of the History and Government Department, Buffalo and Erie County Public Library whose assistance and encouragement have meant so much to me; to Mrs. Virginia E. Currier for the preparation of the manuscript, her enthusiasm and patience; to Mrs. Rebecca Stumm and Mrs. Diane Barber for their able research assistance, and of course, to Mrs. Jean E. Coffey of the Erie County Agricultural Society, for her efforts.

~Ellen Taussig

Creative Arts Department 2001

PRESIDENT	Susan Faulring	
1st V.P.	Pat Burger	Hamburg
Treasurer	Lillian Dunlavey	West Seneca
2nd V.P.	Yvonne Rhodes	Orchard Park
3rd V.P.	Wanda Mergenhagen	West Seneca
4th V.P.	Dolly Kress	Hamburg
Secretary	Alice Say	Hamburg

Directors

Marlene Peters (David)	Orchard Park
Lillian Dunlavey (John)	West Seneca
Marie Nadolny (Eugene)	Elma
Bonnie Schichtel (Dale)	West Falls
Judy Tucholski	Cheektowaga
Patricia Phillips	Hamburg
Claire Faulring	Lawtons
Florence Mergenhagen	East Aurora
Delacy Wood	Tonawanda
Christine Hartmann	East Aurora

Director Emeritus

Patricia Bury	Hamburg
Erie County Fair liason	Jessica Gominiak

Bibliography

Bisco, Jim. "A Greater Look at Greater Buffalo." Northridge, Cal.: Windsor Publication, 1986

Brown, Richard C. and Watson, Bob. Buffalo: "Lake City in the Niagara Land, An Illustrated History." Woodland Hills, Cal.: Windsor Publication, 1981.

Eberle, Scott G. and Grande, Joseph A.: "Second Looks, A Pictorial History of Buffalo and Erie County." Norfolk, Va.: Donning Company, 1987.

"Fairs, U.S.A." Ithaca, N.Y.: Image Digest Inc., 1970.

Goldman, Mark. "High Hopes: The Rise and Decline of Buffalo, New York." Albany: State University Press, 1983.

"The Town of Hamburg Sesquicentennial Reflections Through the Years." Hamburg, N.Y.: Hamburg Sesquicentennial Committee, 1962.

Hedrick, Ulysses Prentiss. "The History of Agriculture in the State of New York." Albany: New York State Agricultural Society, 1933.

Horton, John T., Williams, Edward T., and Douglass, Harry S. "Northwestern New York: Erie, Niagara, Wyoming, Genesee and Orleans Counties." vol. 2. New York: Lewis Historical Publishing Company, 1947.

Johnson, Chrisfield. "Centennial History of Erie County, New York." Buffalo: Matthews and Warren Printers, 1876.

Lyman, J.H. "The Agriculture of Erie Count." Transactions of the New York State Agricultural Society, vol. 3. Albany: Carroll and Cook, Printers to the Assembly, 1843.

McKennon, Joe. "A Pictorial History of the American Carnival." vol. 1. Sarasota, Fla.: Carnival Publishers of Sarasota, 1972.

Minutes of the Erie County Agricultural Society 1856-1895, and intermittent years thereafter.

Neely, Wayne C. "The Agricultural Fair." New York: Columbia University Press, 1935.

Smith, H. Perry, ed. "History of the City of Buffalo and Erie County." 2 vols. Syracuse, N.Y.: D. Mason & Col., 1884.

Transactions of the New York Agricultural Society, Albany: 1842-1896.

West Seneca Centennial Society, Inc. "West Seneca Centennial Celebration – July 15th to 21st 1951."

White, Truman C. "Our County and Its People." A descriptive work on Erie County, N.Y. Boston, Mass.: The Boston History Company Publishers, 1898.

Williams, T. Harry, Current, Richard N. and Freidel, Frank. "A History of the United States Since 1865." New York: Knopf, 1969, 3rd edition.

Papers

Papers, reports, documents and photographs from the files of the Erie County Agricultural Society – 1819 to date.

Memorabilia from the files of George G. Sipprell, former Society treasurer and Fair historian.

Newspapers

Buffalo Business First	Buffalo Commercial Advertiser	Buffalo Courier-Express
Buffalo Daily Courier	Buffalo Evening News	Buffalo Express
Buffalo News	Buffalo Evening Post	Buffalo Times